Awakening Into Perfect Peace

Ralph Huber, Ph.D.

MUSE HARBOR
PUBLISHING

LOS ANGELES SANTA BARBARA

Awakening Into Perfect Peace

A Muse Harbor Publishing Book

PUBLISHING HISTORY

Muse Harbor Publishing print edition
published November 2013

Published by Muse Harbor Publishing, LLC

Los Angeles, California

Santa Barbara, California

All rights reserved, including the right to reproduce this book in whole or in part. For information, contact Muse Harbor Publishing.

Copyright © 2013 by Ralph Huber

ISBN 978-1-61264-139-3

Visit Muse Harbor Publishing at

http://www.museharbor.com

To everything that is.

Contents

Awakened	ix
Preface	xiii
Introduction	xvii

Allowing All of Life to Be as It Is — 1

Vanquishing the Root Problem	3
Ending Our Suffering	6
Graciously Allowing	8
Distinguishing Suffering from Pain	10
Releasing Control	12
Not Believing Our Judgmental Stories	15
Knowing Our "Not-Two" True Nature	17
Questioning Our Thinking	19
Seeing No Mistakes	24
Returning to Resonance	26
Laughing at Our Stories	30
No Wrong-Making	33
Affirming Life's Perfection	37
Living in Compassion	39
Musings	*44*

Yes, Thank You — 47

Giving Thanks for All of Life	49
Focusing on Our Blessings	52
Ending Tyranny's Reign	54
Complaining Won't Help	58
Embracing All Emotions	62

Inviting Curiosity Rather Than Judgment	65
Giving Up the Search	71
Responding from a Grateful Heart	75
Saying the Yes of Peace	82
Musings	*86*

The Three-Step Process for Perfect Peace — 89

Removing Barriers to Peace	91
The Three-Step Process for Perfect Peace Worksheet	99
Musings	*101*

The Illusion of Separation — 103

Going Beyond the Words	105
Knowing Our Oneness	107
Looking Past Appearances	110
Being Lived by Life	112
Identifying No "Me" or "Other"	114
Blaming No One	117
Understanding the Limits of Language	121
Providing Pointers	123
Turning Upside-Down	126
Resisting Nothing	128
Moving Past Dualistic Logic	131
Being Nothing that Is Everything	135
Seeing the World as Illusion	138
Losing Our Attachments	142
Shining Perfect Peace	144
Musings	*145*

Questions and Answers — 147

Musings	*159*

Resources	161
About the Author	169
Acknowledgements	171

Suffering
ceases to be suffering
when we form
a clear picture
of it.

Spinoza

Awakened

Oh, let us rest in
The perfect peace of
Who we truly are–

Beyond all appearances,
All concepts
All notions of a separate self;

Beyond all stories of
Good or bad; right or wrong;
Praise or blame; loss or gain;

With nothing grasped at,
Nothing pushed away,
Nothing special, nor not special.

And no belief that says
Life should be any different
Than life is.

For nothing in this universe runs amiss:
All unfolds perfectly–
Yes, perfectly of its own accord!

Why not, then, just relax
In the mysterious, eternal-knowing
Play of infinite awareness:

This pure, unbridled awareness
Of indivisible love
Where no problem can reside–

Neither lack nor worry,
No story-rooted judgment
Of any suffering kind.

For when we rest
In absolute awareness,
All thoughts that claim

Some life unfoldment is
To us a disadvantage,
We clearly see as misguided thinking.

In Truth, we know ourselves
To always be
Fully loved, fully safe, fully free.

And with this knowing
There co-arises
A grace of ever-giving thanks;

A grace by which we bless–
Again and then again–
The totality of being,

Seeing past its
Many dueling guises
To the benevolent harmony within.

And with this deep according
Pulsing All That Is,
We can wholly be in communion

By fashioning a heart
So singly sourced
In healing forgiveness and perpetual embrace

That all resistance to life,
As life is,
Is surrendered.

Thus freed, we may,
By gift of Spirit, come
To find ourselves awake:

Absent of
All illusory fear;
All imposter guilt

Now newly birthed,
We live afresh in the
Perfect peace of Oneness–

This ineffable not two
Of Oneness–
Who we truly are:

The vast still point
Of pure potential
And unreserved love.

Preface

Awakening Into Perfect Peace is for anyone who desires to live free of suffering—free of stories that argue with life, free of feeling separate from the totality of life. That freedom speaks to this book's purpose, which is to explore the causes of suffering and how to end it. Only when suffering stops can we open to the perfect peace of who we truly are.

About a year ago I completed what I thought was close to a final draft of this book. I was satisfied with the insights I'd gained about how we bring suffering into our lives. However, there seemed to be an overarching piece missing that would effectively weave together the various perspectives offered here.

What was missing remained a mystery until I was asked to give a talk at the Unity Church in Santa Fe. As I was outlining ideas for a talk on how to end our suffering, that missing piece came into view in the form of an acronym—ROAR!

Relax: Allow life to be as life is with a faith-filled surrender that life unfolds perfectly.

Observe: Compassionately notice the suffering that arises from believing life should be different than life is.

Appreciate: Continuously give thanks for all of life from a "Yes, this too!" blessing heart.

Remember: See past all appearances of separation to know our True Nature of infinite love and oneness.

Here was a gestalt to capture the key elements of ending our suffering so that we can live the peace of our True Nature. To test the efficacy of ROAR, I began using it as a tool of inquiry whenever I found myself in the dream of psychological suffering. I'd ask myself:

- Am I allowing life to be as life is with a faith-filled surrender that life unfolds perfectly? (Relax)
- Am I compassionately noticing the suffering that arises from believing life should be different than life is? (Observe)
- Am I continuously giving thanks for all of life from a "Yes, this too!" blessing heart? (Appreciate)
- Am I seeing past all appearances of separation to know our

True Nature of infinite love and oneness? (Remember)

I discovered that when I asked ROAR questions I experienced a relief from my suffering. I became awake. Will Rogers said, "If you find yourself in a hole, quit digging!" ROAR can provide a way to climb out of the hole of suffering so you can begin walking on the path of peace. With this in mind, use ROAR not only as a compass to assist you in navigating through this book, but also as a tool of inquiry: Ask the ROAR questions when you find yourself digging ever deeper into a hole of suffering. Trust that you will discover how quickly you can wake up from your suffering and live in perfect peace.

Introduction

Welcome the world into your arms.

Tao Te Ching

I'd like to invite you to think back to times in your life when you've had less than peaceful, loving feelings. Specifically, when you may have been feeling angry, frustrated, disappointed, depressed, or anxious. What was the root cause of your distress? In each instance, wasn't there a story you were telling yourself that:

> someone in your life should be
>   different than he or she is
> or
> something in your life should be
>   different than it is
> or
> you should somehow be
>   different than you are.

For example:

- My boss shouldn't be so critical of my work.
- My roommate should clean up after she eats and not leave a bunch of dirty dishes in the sink.
- My co-workers should be more responsible.
- I should be thinner/smarter/more popular.
- Life shouldn't be so damned hard.
- It shouldn't be raining cats and dogs on the very day I arranged for a family picnic in the park.
- My heating bill shouldn't be so high.
- My children should pick up their clothes.

Why does telling "Life should be different than it is" stories result in feelings of distress?

Well, that's because your True Nature doesn't tell any such stories. Your True Nature proclaims in every moment an unequivocal yes to life, offering an affirming, welcoming embrace to life in all its aspects. Who you really are, your True Nature, doesn't do right or wrong, good or bad, thumbs up or thumbs down. Rather, your True Nature in its perfect love and oneness is free of judgment about anything. There is in your True Nature no possibility for drama, or any roller coaster of emotions; nor any place for sackcloth and ashes or mea culpas. Instead, there is an all-encompassing silence—free of any story—that is ocean-deep in stillness.

Your True Nature loves you
exactly as you are,

loves others exactly as they are and

loves life exactly as it is!

Given that spirit of embracing rather than resisting life, your True Nature is unable to hold any should/shouldn't judgments about life. And so when we harbor a judgment—tell a story—that life should somehow be different than it is, we are out of resonance with our True Nature. It's our being out of resonance with our True Nature that gives rise to stressful feelings such as anger, frustration, and worry.

Can you see that?

Take a moment and imagine saying "*Yes*, thank you!" to everything in your life, regardless of what shows up. The unconditional *yes* of your True Nature. A welcoming *yes* that proclaims your openness to allowing all of life to be as it is.

What would your experience be living such a life? Would you feel at peace? Relaxed? Free of moral judgments of good or bad; right or wrong? Flowing with life rather than fighting it? Honoring your preferences with a light touch instead of being stressed with tight-fisted must-have's?

Such a life is readily available when we stay in resonance with our True Nature, saying *yes* to life rather than demanding life show up a certain way. Indeed, the principal point you'll find emphasized in this book is that our resistance to how life is unfolding is the primary roadblock to our experiencing the perfect peace of our True Nature.

This book has five parts. Part I discusses how we get out of resonance with our True Nature and bring suffering upon ourselves by resisting rather than embracing life. Part II continues to look at the self-inflicted suffering we experience when believing in our stories that oppose life. Part III gives a three-step process to assist us in questioning the truth of our judgmental should thoughts. This process shapes the ROAR perspectives offered in the Preface into a powerful mode of inquiry that can deepen our insights into the causes of suffering and strengthen our ability to end it.

Part IV focuses on how understanding the loving-oneness of our True Nature can liberate us from needing life to fit our picture of how we think it ought to unfold. Part V gives answers to the most often asked questions about waking up to the perfect peace of our True Nature.

In exploring this book's invitation to free ourselves of our psychological suffering, it's important to note that language in its dualism is inherently limited, created by our geared-for-survival egoic self. Consequently, the survival-driven egoic self could judge the perspectives presented here as threats to its existence and will urge you to dismiss them as wrong-headed, nonsensical, and even dangerous. The ego might voice a warning like, "Don't be so foolish as to give up your belief in your judgmental stories. To survive in this world, you need to listen to those stories, even if they bring you anger, anxiety, frustration, irritation, depression and illness!"

Don't listen to what your egoic self is telling you. Go beyond it as you read this book, remaining open to the ideas presented here. Be assured that as you commit to staying in resonance with your True Nature you will dramatically strengthen your ability to live the perfect peace that is who you really are.

I

Allowing All of Life to Be as It Is

> Declare a cease-fire on the war
> with reality: allow, let it be.
>
> *Elizabeth Hamilton*

Vanquishing the Root Problem

There once was a king who greatly suffered, feeling trapped in endless mental turmoil. He couldn't abide all the quarreling of his ministers; the contrary nature of his wife, the queen; the slowly sinking treasury; the inability to get a restful night's sleep; and the inordinate laziness of his son, the prince. This and much more he suffered.

And so when he heard of a wise monk in his kingdom who people praised for helping them attain inner peace, he commanded the monk to come see him. When the monk came, the king immediately voiced his litany of problems. The monk listened intently, and when the king finished speaking, the monk said,

"I cannot help you with any of the problems you've mentioned."

Upon hearing this, the king grew very upset and said, "What do you mean by saying that? What good are you to me if you can't help me with my problems?"

The monk replied, "Sire, we each have 56 problems in our lives. Even if I could take care of each of your 56 problems, 56 additional problems would quickly take their place."

"But I don't understand," said the king, "You have a reputation for solving people's problems!"

"I do not solve any of the 56 problems people have, sire. Instead, I help people to stop believing in what they may not see as their 57th problem," said the monk.

"What is this 57th problem," asked the king.

The monk replied, "The 57th problem is believing that life should be different than it is."

The monk continued, "My most humble counsel to you, sire, is to stop believing in the 57th problem, then all of what you believe are your other problems will vanish like a morning mist."

The king replied, "I don't understand what you mean."

"Sire," continued the monk, "we suffer to the extent that we believe in our stories which oppose life. Vanquish those stories and you will be graced in allowing all of life to be as it is, not as you believe it should be. Then the peace you are seeking will be yours."

The king paused for a great while and then bowing humbly to the monk said, "All you have told me penetrates my heart. You speak the highest wisdom."

This story of the monk and the king expresses a core message of this book—the way to experience true inner peace and happiness in our lives is to allow life to be as it is. And we can only do that if we stop believing the judgmental stories about life that we fashion in our minds.

> …if you're judging from the way you think things should be, then problems arise.
>
> Bob Adamson

Ending Our Suffering

Let's take the king in our story and imagine how his many problems would vanish by not believing in his judgmental stories that life should be different than it is. Without those stories, the king would cease to give himself anguish by resisting life's natural unfoldment. The king—no longer telling himself judgmental stories about life—could then be with his queen, his son, his ministers, his nightly sleep, and his treasury from a place of inner peace that is free of demands that life show up in a certain way.

Now certainly the king would still take action in his world. Residing in inner peace doesn't mean one becomes inert, passively underfoot to life. Rather, by allowing life to be as it is, he could then open to his heart's intelligence and have that be the source for his actions—actions that wouldn't be colored with struggle and stress. In short, the king's path to freedom from suffering, as is ours, is an internal, not external path; that is, the path of questioning the truth of our judgmental stories about life.

Graciously Allowing

Allow is a key word used throughout this book. How is *allow* meant be understood? The word *allow* as in the sentence "Allow all of life to be as it is" is intended to be viewed as holding a spirit of an effortless welcoming, a *yes* to life.

Sometimes people use the word *allow* in a manner that connotes a reluctant resignation—"Okay, I'll allow you to do that, but I don't think it's right." Using *allow* in this way maintains a distinct flavor of resistance. That is not how *allow* is to be understood here.

When it's said to *allow all of life to be as it is*, there's an intention to convey a full affirming of life—a story-free flowing with life instead of a resistance to it. To help indicate this way of holding the word *allow*, you'll find the word *gracious* often teamed with the word *allow* in this book, as in *gracious allowing*.

> Simply allow "what is" and
> the ground of love will
> emerge to embrace you.
>
> Tony Parsons

Distinguishing Suffering from Pain

There may be no more puzzling or poignant inquiry than *What is at the root of our suffering?* Is it something outside of ourselves acting upon us, victimizing us? Or is it some mental position we take that results in such *dis*easing feelings as worry, anger, frustration, and depression? To answer this question, it's important to first distinguish suffering from pain, as presented in this book.

Suffering is the psychological distress we experience when thinking about some aspect of our lives that we tell ourselves isn't right. Pain, on the other hand, is the physical distress we feel from some bodily disorder—a cut on one's hand would result in pain, but not necessarily suffering.

A mental judgment of a cut on one's hand such as "What an idiot I was to be so careless with that knife! I'm so damned clumsy," and lingering on that mind-created story can bring on the suffering we're talking about.

It's important not to confuse these two experiences—suffering, which is mental distress, and pain, which is physical distress.

> Pain is inevitable.
> Suffering is not.
>
> *Jack Kornfield*

Releasing Control

Consider some of the truly great spiritual teachers such as the Buddha, Christ, Lao Tzu, and Meister Eckhart plus in more recent times Ramana Maharshi and Nisargadatta Maharaj. What you'll find when looking at their lives is that instead of wrestling with life, attempting to get life under control, they let go and flowed with life.

Living in this spirit of allowing rather than resistance, life was able to freely move through them. They lived fearless lives of inner peace by not holding any suffering stories about how life wasn't perfect as it is.

This doesn't mean that by flowing with life these great masters passively sat around in a blissed-out state all day; they took action in the world to the degree they felt called. However, their actions weren't fired by a desire to control life. Why would they desire to control life when they weren't telling themselves any stories about how life was imperfect? The peace these masters experienced we can also experience when we let go of our demands upon life.

> Nothing has to be achieved in order to be at peace. All we have to do is…stop getting upset when things don't go as we would wish, or when people don't behave as we think they should.
>
> *Peter Russell*

When we let go of trying to control life and instead allow all of life to be as it is, we sense that life is for us, not against us, and that we are being graced with a continual flow of blessings.

To better understand the nature of this particularly peaceful way of being in the world, it's helpful to spend time looking at those feelings that contrast the peace of allowing. Consider those instances when we are distressed, feeling emotions like frustration, worry, boredom, and just plain irritation. When emotionally in *dis*ease, it's likely that we don't see life as being on our side or that blessings are streaming our way. When feeling contracted and stressed, we may believe that circumstances outside of ourselves are the cause of our stress. We expect life "out there" to show up a certain way and it's not!

One might believe, for instance, that stress results from...*that slow driver in front of me; the neighbor who keeps his porch light on all night that shines right into my bedroom window; my computer, which has sent into its intractable bowels the time-critical document I was working on.*

Well, the truth of the matter is that the stress we feel in life is not caused by our life circumstances but rather by the stories we tell ourselves about those circumstances.

Not Believing Our Judgmental Stories

When we believe our judgmental stories about life, stress can quickly show up. Stories, for instance, like the following:

- People should be more respectful.
- TV shows shouldn't show so much violence.
- Politicians should be more honest.
- My neighbors should pick up the trash in their yard.
- My adult children shouldn't be asking me for money all the time.

- There shouldn't be genocide and war and poverty and hunger and...

Most people's list of "life isn't right" stories are endless and as a result they live in a continual stream of discontent. The way out of this discontent? *Don't believe in your stories that argue with life.*

Why do stories that argue with life create emotional stress? Well, when we are busy *shoulding*...

on ourselves (*I should be thinner*);
on others (*My sister should be more thoughtful*);
or on life in general (*It shouldn't be so cold this time of year*)...

we are out of resonance with the very ground of our being—our True Nature—which never takes issue with life.

When we believe our stories of complaint about life, we are in resistance to the unfolding of life, while our True Nature, which is who we truly are, is at complete peace with life. *Our True Nature can only allow life to be as it is.*

Knowing Our "Not-Two" True Nature

Our True Nature is free of conditioned mind structures of good/bad, right/wrong stories. Further, our True Nature of infinite love and oneness is unchanging. Thus, our True Nature isn't our physical appearance, our thoughts, beliefs, possessions, opinions, expectations, income, education, or heritage: anything you can name that isn't permanent is not who you really are.

Our True Nature in its infinite stillness is nothing and everything, timeless and spaceless—and thus cannot tell stories of any kind. How can something that is undivided ever tell a story—what would this that is undivided tell a story about since there is nothing other than the undivided? You need two to tell a story, to have a conflict, to put up a resistance; and our True Nature is not two.

> The heart of the mystic discovery is that we are all one and that One is unconditioned, unlimited and undefined.
>
> *Beatrice Bruteau*

Questioning Our Thinking

No story that argues with reality is true. Each one is an imposter, a made-up story of how life needs/must/has to be different for you to be at peace with the world. Fully taking this in is critical if we're going to be able to drop our belief in stress-producing thoughts that promote hard and fast expectations about life.

Let's say it's late evening and you're walking out in the desert and you see a snake coiled up not three feet away. You become alarmed but when you take a closer look you see that it's not a snake but rather a coiled up piece of rope.

What happens? Do you stay alert and on guard? Of course not. Because what you first believed to be true, isn't! Your belief in the story "It's a snake!" naturally drops away. You don't have to make the story drop away because you see that your story isn't true.

Similarly when you see the untruth in any stress-producing story, the story simply falls on its own. You don't have to push it over the cliff, drown it, or beat it into the dirt. However, if you continued to believe the rope was actually a snake, there's no way the story "It's a snake!" could drop away.

> It can be consoling
> to discover that you
> don't have to believe in
> your own thoughts.
>
> *John Tarrant*

When you're feeling stressed, you can use the formula below to identify the story you're creating so that you can then shed light on its untruth:

For me to be at peace ____X____ *should (or shouldn't)* ___Y___.

Here are some examples:

- For me to be at peace my boss should appreciate me more.
- For me to be at peace I should lose twenty pounds.
- For me to be at peace Tibet should be free of Chinese oppression.
- For me to be at peace life should be easier.
- For me to be at peace tsunamis shouldn't happen.
- For me to be at peace my parents should have loved me more.

Once you've identified your story, then you can begin to question it and see how stressing yourself by resisting the reality of what is isn't helpful. And why isn't it helpful to resist? Because what you're resisting isn't true!

Invariably what happens when we're stressing ourselves is that we're believing some story about how life isn't quite right...

that life is making a mistake being as it is...
that life is sadly mixed up in how
   it's arranging things...
that life is having moments of madness.

And someone viewing life in this way might say something like the following: "*Well, isn't it true there shouldn't be poverty, or disease, or illiteracy, or genocide, or orphans, or dictators, or hurricanes that leave death and destruction in their wake, or my neighbor who parks her eyesore of a car in front of my house when I've asked her not to?*"

We may as well face it...in this world, there is poverty and disease and illiteracy and recalcitrant neighbors and all the rest. (Remember: Our True Nature allows *everything*—cute puppy dogs, gorgeous sunsets, as well as destitution and life "red in tooth and claw.") So doesn't fighting with what is—angrily waving our list of demands—seem to be an overwhelming battle we're sure to be engaged in without end? Isn't there always something out there in the world that we believe needs to be fixed?

Given that reality is as it is, wouldn't a kinder, more compassionate approach be to drop our resistance to what is and then take action from a place of inner peace rather than inner strife? What we don't have to do is hold onto our complaints about life in such a tight-fisted way that we experience stress and struggle. What we can do is turn our list of complaints and demands into a list of preferences, which then frees us from needing x, y, or z to happen for us to be at peace.

Some people believe that they need to feel the stress of wrong-making to propel them into right action. Not so. We can take action from a place of peace without diminishing our capacity to act. What we may find is that our actions have greater efficacy in the long run when we're not taking action in resistance to life.

Seeing No Mistakes

Your True Nature knows that resistance to what is doesn't help! Your True Nature knows that all of life is perfectly unfolding because life could not unfold in any other way. One might say that your True Nature is continuously vibrating *All is Perfect as It Is*. Your True Nature doesn't complain about life. Your True Nature is unbounded, unlimited, lacking in any particle of desire to control life, free of any demands about how life needs to be.

Remember, your True Nature is undivided—one, not two; how life unfolds is simply how life unfolds. And in truth, it's more accurate to say that for your True Nature, *life unfolds neither perfectly nor imper-*

fectly—life simply unfolds as it unfolds. Further—and this your egoic self can't intellectually grasp—there's not even any life unfolding since your True Nature is unchanging and absent of any form.

And so when you believe in a story such as *life should be fair,* you are in a vibration that is exactly opposite from your True Nature. With stories that question how life is unfolding, you are saying that *All is not Perfect as It Is,* that there's a mistake happening and something needs to change and be put aright. As a result, you feel *dis*eased because your True Nature sees no mistake, no flaw, nothing that needs to be changed, improved, fixed, corrected—nothing that needs to be excluded from life!

Returning to Resonance

Let's examine one of the stressful stories previously presented and see how it's actually a fantasy.

Story: *For me to be at peace my boss should appreciate me more.* (And for the purposes of our inquiry, consider this a story in which you believe.)

What's the reality of this story that your boss should appreciate you more? The reality is that your boss appreciates you as much as your boss does. That's the reality, stripped of story. Believing that your boss should appreciate you more is delusional. Can you see that?

Your True Nature can.

Your True Nature is at peace with the way your boss appreciates—or doesn't appreciate—you. Your True Nature, by its very essence, embraces all of life—"unappreciative" bosses included. There's no judgment in your True Nature, no attempts to control life, no yearning for life to be other than it is—in sum, no wrong-making because your True Nature is at total ease with life. Therefore, believing in a story that your boss should appreciate you more puts you out of step with your all-embracing True Nature. As a result suffering happens!

> Who said that the way
> life naturally unfolds
> is not all right?
>
> *Michael A. Singer*

Your True Nature is at perfect peace with life. Your True Nature wouldn't have life show up any other way. Rather than believing in a story that argues with reality such as *my boss should appreciate me more,* you can get back in harmony with your True Nature by saying something like, *"I'm appreciated by my boss to the extent that I'm appreciated. And what I can do is to appreciate myself the way I want to be appreciated."*

Doesn't that feel more peaceful and life-giving? Why is that? Because there's a return to resonance with one's True Nature. There's not a buying into the delusional belief that something in life needs to change to alleviate your suffering.

Given that your True Nature is in love with reality as it is, we can say that rather than being distressed about anything that is happening in life your True Nature is pure relaxation. When you are relaxed with life—and not caught up in believing stories that contradict life—an open communion with your True Nature naturally happens.

Relaxation dissolves our mental critic so that we can savor all the shades and textures of life. Our sense of humor comes to our aid; we can laugh at ourselves and at life's seeming mishaps from a wider perspective. When we are relaxed with life, we are at peace even when life seems to be throwing us curve balls. Notice how very friendly life becomes when we fully let go and relax.

If there were a technique
that could bring about
liberation I would put it in
one word. I would say 'Relax.'

Richard Sylvester

Laughing at Our Stories

Ask yourself this question: Do I want to experience the well-being that comes from deep inner peace?

Stop for a moment and fully relax into this question.

How strong is your desire to live the perfect peace of your True Nature? Is it with all of your being? With all of your fully relaxed being? Not striving? Not coming from a place of lack? Can you now see yourself saying when you are suffering *"Ah, suffering! I must be believing an insane story that life should be different than it is. How interesting to notice this. How laughable to believe in a story that isn't true."*

To notice what's really behind your suffering and to be relaxed in that noticing is the necessary first step in order to experience the peace to which we're pointing. Do you feel encouraged now that you understand a primary source of suffering, and that by relaxing with life—allowing life to be as it is—you can end the suffering?

> You will escape suffering
> only to the degree you are
> willing and able to be okay
> with whatever happens.
> People who live by rules,
> shoulds, or have-to's tend
> to suffer quite often.
>
> *Bill Harris*

Imagine for a moment the peace you would give yourself by releasing your stories that judge life when life doesn't suit your picture of how you want it to unfold. Imagine how much softer the conversations you hold with yourself in your mind would be. How much more at ease you would be physically. How much more fulfilling and harmonious your relationships would be with others and life.

As written in the *Tao Te Ching*:

> The hard and rigid
> will be broken.
> The soft and supple
> will prevail.

When we resist life, we become rigid in our mind, body and spirit. When we say *yes* to life, we can relax into the flow of life with an easy grace, opening ourselves to what wants to happen, knowing that life in its infinite wisdom holds the big picture.

No Wrong-Making

This doesn't mean that in being open to life we are giving our stamp of approval to everything that's happening; nor does it mean that we become a doormat for life. We still move out of the way if we find ourselves in the path of a speeding truck. We still have preferences, but we hold our preferences lightly. We still set boundaries when they're called for, but not with a club in hand.

For example, one might say to someone who isn't handing in work projects on time something like this:

Yes, I understand that you're feeling sorry again for not getting a project to me on time. I find I work better when time agreements are kept, and I think that we may not be a match to work together on projects that involve time agreements. What do you think?

Notice that there's no blaming, no wrong-making. There's simply a realization that continuing down a particular path doesn't seem to be working at this time. In short, we realize that we feel moved to make a course correction free of any "This is wrong, bad, or unfair" judgments. Also notice the person speaking in this example is fully respecting a preference held about time agreements. We all have our preferences that support us as we move through life; to get rid of our preferences wouldn't prove practical.

It's helpful, for instance, to have a preference that when you hire a lawn service, they will take care of your yard. Without any preference, you may as well hire a plumber or a lawyer. What's not helpful is when we turn our preferences into demands and make another wrong for not respecting our preferences.

In the time agreements example above, the person doesn't go into wrong-making by saying something like, "It shows a lack of responsibility to not keep your time agreements. Why can't you be more considerate of others?"

When we go into wrong-making, we are out of tune with our True Nature that sees no mistakes and therefore banishes nothing in life—not war, not pestilence, not disease, not genocide, not environmental degradation, unkept time agreements, or anything else we view as amiss in the world.

> There really is no good
> or bad, right or wrong.
>
> *Gina Mazza Hillier*

When we refrain from wrong-making and say *yes* to life, we keep open to our inner guidance. Absent are any dictates about how we or others should act.

For instance, we give ourselves the freedom to decline invitations around which we don't feel integrity in accepting: "I appreciate that you've asked me to participate in the school fund-raising event again this year, but I've made a commitment to spend more time with my family instead of taking on other activities."

Remember, our openness to how life is unfolding doesn't mean we simply resign ourselves to whatever is happening, ignoring any impulse to take action regarding a situation that calls up a response in us. If I hear of a disaster happening to people either close to home or on the other side of the world and feel moved to respond in some way, I can send prayers as well as contribute a donation to the appropriate relief organization. Or let's say I read an article about the vanishing rain forests in South America. I may feel called to become a member of an environmental group that is dedicated to making a difference in that part of the world.

The point here is that I take action from a peaceful place of accepting what is. That's the reality of life in this moment. And I relax myself into life by graciously allowing life to be as it is. In that allowing I can then take action free of any stress-inducing moral demands: *"This shouldn't be happening; this is wrong, bad, evil, horrible, not right,"* and so on.

We will find that when we refrain from story-making about how life is in error, we can move in the world with clarity and grace rather than confusion and struggle. Our thinking and speaking is reasoned and rational while being informed by an intuitive and understanding heart. We become wary of any promptings to imbue our words and actions with rigid self-righteousness or an arrogance that says "I know best!" We live in humility, not attempting to force life to show up in a certain way.

Affirming Life's Perfection

We find that when we take action from a place of humility, we give ourselves an experience that is markedly different from that of taking action with an attitude of "I know best!" Let us ask ourselves: "Do I want to cultivate a life experience of confusion and drama by an arrogant resistance to life?" Or, "Do I want to cultivate a life of wisdom and peace that comes from a humble embrace of life's perfect unfoldment?"

It's worth noting that the word *perfect* as used above is not to be viewed in a dualistic sense of good compared to bad. Rather, in the spirit of this discussion *perfect* connotes wholeness, completeness, and without division. For instance, something can be a perfect delight or a perfect disaster. In this sense *perfect* conveys an impeccability to what is occurring because that is in fact what's occurring. Thus, life is perfect as it is from the perspective that that's how life is showing up. To judge it as somehow bad or blemished can only give rise to suffering.

To view life's perfection in this way doesn't mean that we applaud what's happening or refrain from taking any action if we feel so moved. Life continually courses through us and action will in most cases eventually occur regardless of our attitude; it's just that the action that flows from a spirit of allowing life's perfect unfoldment will be imbued with grace rather than struggle.

> All suffering results from
> your refusal to accept and
> bless life just the way it is….
> There is nothing lacking,
> nothing insufficient, nothing
> broken. It is perfect as it is.
>
> *Paul Ferrini*

Living in Compassion

The Dalai Lama is an inspiring example of someone who takes action from a place of inner peace, rooted in his gracious allowing of life. Given all that has happened to him, his people and his country over the years, he consistently refrains from expressing any hatred toward the communist Chinese.

At a fund raising event where I saw him speak, he clearly spoke of the assaults the people of Tibet were suffering and asked for our support. However, there was no rancor, no blaming, no judgment, no intimation of ill-will in his voice. No hint of him making the Chinese wrong.

The peace the Dalai Lama radiated was cast in bold relief when compared to the introductory talk given by the woman who helped organize the benefit. Her words were sharp and critical, her demeanor very tight and agitated. She characterized the communist Chinese as villains of the first order. She was fully wrapped in her judgmental stories about the Chinese. As I listened to her speak, I wondered what the Dalai Lama felt about her harsh words. I could imagine his compassion for the suffering she was inflicting on herself with her judgments and accusations.

> I feel that compassionate thought
> is the most precious thing there is.
>
> *The Dalai Lama*

Following that event I read an interview in which the Dalai Lama was asked how he could remain at peace, considering all the tragedy that had befallen him and Tibet. He replied that his country had been taken away from him, but that didn't mean he was going to let his peace be taken away. In other words, he wasn't going to get caught up in a finger-pointing drama, railing against the Chinese and their actions towards him and his country.

In the same spirit of this story about the Dalai Lama, here's a story the psychologist and author Daniel Goleman tells:

The setting is a subway car in Japan. A friend of Goleman's who's trained in the martial art of aikido sees a drunken, disheveled man enter the subway car, angrily flailing his arms and shouting. He nearly hits some people, creating havoc among the passengers; Goleman's friend, who had previously been something of a brawler in his life, thinks that now might be the perfect opportunity to use his aikido training and put the drunkard in his place.

When he begins to approach the drunken man, the man fiercely announces to the people in the subway car that he's going to teach this foreigner a lesson. As the drunken man moves to attack, Goleman's friend hears a loud but friendly voice say, "Hey."

The comradely voice comes from a small, elderly Japanese man, wearing a kimono. The elderly man raises a hand and beckons the drunken man to come over to him. The drunken man replies, "Why the hell should I talk to you?"

The elderly man asks, "What'cha been drinking?" The drunken man replies, "Sake, and it's none of your business."

Then the elderly man begins to speak about how much he enjoys drinking sake in his garden, and creates in his description a scene of such peace and tranquility that the drunken man's belligerency begins washing away.

The elderly man says how much he enjoys drinking sake with his wonderful wife, and asks the drunken man about his wife. The drunken man says with tears that his wife has died, that he has lost his job, and that he has no home and is so ashamed of himself. The drunken man then sits down next to the elderly man and lays his head in the elderly man's lap.

Goleman's friend, now humbled as he looks on, realizes that putting the drunken man in his place wasn't what was called for. He sees the healing power that comes from taking action in a spirit of compassion rather than judgment.

As we take to heart this story along with the example of the Dalai Lama, let's question the belief that we need our harsh judgments to propel us into righting the "wrongs" in the world. Might not action that emerges from a compassionate embrace of life—and thus resting in the peace of one's True Nature—result in action that's even more effective and healing?

> Being more kind and
> compassionate toward
> all beings and speaking
> lovingly to others is
> ultimately the path of
> the human being.
>
> *Dennis Genpo Merzel*

Musings

Allowing life to be as life is——rather than demanding that life be a certain way——is a key spiritual principle. Life doesn't always unfold exactly as we'd like it to; life simply is as it is. Can we relax in that knowing?

Even my darkest moments contain a bright and peaceful light when I release my attachment to what I believe should be happening.

Whatever you judge amiss in life you separate from, and separation is a misconception that leads to suffering.

You invite misery into your life by wanting to fix others.

Do you automatically believe your distressing stories about life? If you do, you open the door to discontent.

Can you see that you do not suffer because of the way other people act, but rather from your own self-created stories about their actions? Can you see there is no suffering ready to come out and grab you in any life experience? With this insight comes peace.

What more enlightening sentiment could one hold than, "Life shows up the way it shows up?" I'm most truly awake when I leave it at that, not entering into an arrogant imagining of how I think life needs to show up. That doesn't mean never taking action to bring about change; just don't take action from a belief that there's something wrong. Aspire to take action from a sense of unity rather than separation.

If I'm at war with life, I cannot create peace.

Life, in its perfection, doesn't give you everything you crave.

The perfect people and circumstances show up in my life in the perfect way and at the perfect time——no exceptions.

II

Yes, Thank You

There are hundreds of ways to
kneel and kiss the earth.

Rumi

Giving Thanks for All of Life

About 150 years ago there lived a highly revered Zen master named Sono. People would come to Sono and tell her about the challenges they were facing, such as bad health, no money and failed relationships. Sono's response to every person was the same:

"Thank you for everything.

I have no complaint whatsoever."

It wouldn't come as a surprise to learn that not everyone was happy with Sono's response. More than a few became upset, believing that she didn't understand the problems they were facing. How could she say that their challenges were something to be thankful for? Those, however, who truly grasped the wisdom Sono was offering and began to consciously live from a place of unconditional gratitude and non-complaint, reaped the reward of her advice.

What happens when we make a commitment to take up Sono's invitation to welcome all of life with gratitude? As we give thanks for life as it is, we find ourselves relaxing with life rather than resisting life with complaints about how life isn't measuring up. As we give thanks, we find ourselves resting in the perfect peace of our True Nature that says "yes" to life in every moment.

> *"Yes, thank you!"*
> *Always "yes";*
> *always "thank you!"*

The eighteenth century poet and mystic William Blake authored a poem with the phrase "mind-forged manacles." We might view this phrase as pointing to the restraints we create in our minds with our many complaints about life. When we tell ourselves stories that say *no* to what is—reflecting sentiments such as *I don't accept this, I'm at odds with this, he/she/they/I should be different*—we clamp ourselves in mental chains.

What Sono offers is a way to break free with her elegantly simple invitation to give unequivocal thanks for all of life all the time. As the mystic Meister Eckhart wrote, "If the only prayer you ever said was 'Thank you,' that would suffice." When we give thanks for life in every moment, we find ourselves free of suffering; we live the peace of our True Nature—a peace that surpasses all understanding.

> The nineteenth-century Hindu mystic Ramakrishna used to say often: "You can see how evolved someone is from how grateful they are for all the gifts of God."
>
> *Andrew Harvey*

Focusing on Our Blessings

There is no more powerful way to begin a prayer than with "Thank you." When we give thanks for all the good that we already possess, then more good follows.

For example, a way to improved health is to feel gratitude for the areas of good health you currently experience. A way to have more loving relationships in your life is to feel gratitude for those relationships that you experience as especially nurturing and fulfilling.

What you focus on increases. When you focus on what you feel grateful for, more blessings flow your way. And conversely, when you focus on what you feel is lacking in your life, more lack follows—perhaps not in the same area of your life, but lack will show up. If you're feeling negatively about an event in your life and you continue to dwell on it, you are asking for more of that kind of negative vibration to manifest in your life. On the other hand, if you look for something about the event to be grateful for, or focus your attention on some other area of your life that you appreciate, you set the stage for the manifestation of more blessings.

Your True Nature responds to your vibrations: Whatever the feeling tone of your vibration will bounce back to you—call it the "boomerang effect."

Take a moment to consider how your life would be different if, instead of sending out vibrations of lack, you made a commitment to send out vibrations of gratitude, blessing all of life from a thankful heart.

> By giving authentic thanks for all the good you now have, as well as the challenges…you'll start the flow of more good into your life.
>
> Wayne Dyer

Ending Tyranny's Reign

Whenever we resist life, demanding that it change to fit our picture of how we believe it should be unfolding, we sentence ourselves to living under *The Tyranny of Should*. We make our peace of mind dependent upon life showing up the way we want it. When we live under this tyranny, we program our internal radar to constantly scan for instances of how life is falling short. This isn't to say that we aren't allowed to have preferences in our lives. It's when those preferences turn into demands that we set ourselves up for stress.

The Tyranny of Should sees stress as an invitation to bend life to our will so that it will match our vision of what we want to happen, all in the hope of regaining our lost happiness and peace. Seldom do our actions to commandeer life work to our satisfaction. Life has its own plans in mind. And even when our actions do appear to fashion life to our tastes, we fail in the long run. There's always another "life isn't right" experience in the wings, waiting to step into the spotlight, setting the stage for another battle. Clearly not a peaceful way to live. Feeling the impulse to change a situation isn't in itself stress producing. Rather, we give ourselves stress when we oppose life. For example, if I'm feeling cold and a sweater is handy, I can put on the sweater and adjust the thermostat in the room. I don't need to spend time complaining about how it shouldn't be so cold and cause myself stress, unless I'm a diehard complainaholic—in which case I might launch into an inner soliloquy of how it should be warmer at this time of year with spring so close, and how heating costs are rising and how those costs should be lower, but big oil isn't about to let that happen, with their CEO's who should be ashamed of themselves with their outrageous salaries…and how my sweater that I just put on shouldn't be fraying at the sleeves, which goes to show how terrible the quality is in manufactured products these days.

Living in this kind of stream of complaint isn't the way to peace. All this mental chatter about what's wrong with the world and the people in it can only result in continued struggle and drama. How could it be otherwise, given that the emotional turmoil we create in our minds by saying *no* to life puts us out of step with our True Nature that unconditionally embraces life.

While we may not be in the class of the complaint-addicted person described above, if we're honest with ourselves, we'll probably find that a fair portion of our day is spent dipping in and out of a pool of discontent, wishing life were different than it is. For example when we find ourselves in challenging situations, do we start grousing about life and taking on the role of victim, repeatedly asking, "Why me? Why this? Why now?" Or do we find ourselves saying something like: "How interesting that life is showing up in this way. I'm going to keep my focus on how I can creatively deal with this situation."

A foundational attitude for us to adopt in order to experience the peace of our True Nature is that life is perfect as it is. By affirming the perfection of life, we can relax with life—and action, free of stress, naturally arises.

Suffering happens when
you believe thoughts that
tell you that something
should be happening other
than what is happening.

Scott Kiloby

Complaining Won't Help

In eighteenth century Japan there lived the monk and poet Ryokan, who came home to find that a robber had entered his humble hut and stolen his few meager possessions. In response he wrote the following haiku:

> The thief left it behind—
> the moon
> At the window.

Notice how Ryokan didn't mention the physical possessions that were now missing from his hut. He focused instead on what he still had: the moon he saw at his window, which no robber could steal and what Ryokan held as more precious than his stolen possessions.

Consider what kind of haiku Ryokan might have written had he created a story that he shouldn't have been robbed. Perhaps it would have read something like this:

> That dastardly thief
> he stole all *my* things
> Why me, Damn it?

This imagined haiku conveys sentiments that most people would probably express if a thief had entered their home and made away with their belongings: "Curse that thief! I shouldn't have been robbed! Why did this have to happen to me?" When we get ourselves caught in stories like this, we not only have the challenging situation to deal with, but on top of that we add self-inflicted suffering—a suffering that is a direct result of our giving energy to a story about how life has injured us.

Ryokan didn't bring suffering upon himself. He didn't keep replaying in his mind the robbery, which was a single event. Had Ryokan, however, become lost in lamenting his fate, he most probably would have continued to "rob" himself time and again in his imagination. Who then would have been doing Ryokan more violence—the thief or himself? Consider how often we bring suffering upon ourselves by becoming like a hamster running on its wheel, spinning over and over our stories of complaint: *That driver shouldn't have cut me off. My downstairs neighbor shouldn't play her music so loud. My boss should be more sensitive to how much work he loads on me. My son should be more responsible.*

When we become addicted to complaining about life, we imprison ourselves in suffering and victimhood, sometimes for years, with stories like "My older sister should have loved me more." The way out of our self-imposed imprisonment is clear: Question our belief in the story. Then from a place of viewing life's perfection, we can say "My older sister loved me the way she loved me. What I can do is love myself the way I want to be loved." All the energy we spend believing in our stories that I/others/life should be any different, blocks our ability to respond to life in a way that helps us live in peace.

> We suffer more from
> our stories than from the
> actual situation as it is.
>
> *Toni Packer*

Embracing All Emotions

Given what's been presented here, one might conclude that a perpetual Cheshire Cat grin is the ideal being advocated, no matter what one is experiencing in life. That's not the case. It's understandable that we might feel sad, angry, or disappointed over a loss. All feelings are precious and not something to push away; it's not helpful to think that we should at all times and in all situations sport a toothsome smile with a lilting song in our hearts.

There's an instructive story of a monk who was out walking one day and saw his master sobbing by the river. He was stunned to find his master so distressed.

He said, "Master, what is wrong? Why are you crying so?"

His master replied, "My beloved dog, who has been such a faithful companion to me for many years, has died this morning."

"But, Master," said the monk, "You have always taught that this dream-life is impermanent and have spoken so often of the illusion of attachments."

"Yes, that is true. I have taught that," the master said, letting out another sob.

"I don't understand, then," said the monk. "Why are you crying so?"

"Because I am sad," said the master.

What this story beautifully conveys is that having an awareness of life's fleeting nature and the sadness that can come from our attachments to the delights of this world—however illusory—does not mean we should strive to become a stone, unaffected by the loss of that which we hold dear. Being grateful for all of life means embracing every emotion we feel—not just the joyful emotions but also the sad ones as well.

Imagine how sterile and one-dimensional the master in this story would be if, when his beloved dog had died, he simply went about his daily routine as if nothing had happened. Our lives take many twists and turns. To present ourselves to the world as if none of this makes any difference one way or the other denies our very humanity. When I think of this story I see the master fully embracing his sadness, and at the same time I imagine him feeling great appreciation for the gift of loving companionship between him and his dog. Appreciation and sadness are not mutually exclusive emotions.

A friend of mine whose mother was in a coma during the final hours of her life told me how grateful he felt to sit beside her, gently stroking her arm and speaking softly to her about all the beauty and blessings she had experienced in her life. His sadness at her physical leave taking and his feeling of gratitude to be with her at this most sacred and precious time were profoundly united. He hadn't experienced anything in his life more poignant or beautiful.

In both my friend's experience and that of the master who lost his beloved companion, there's no indication that they thought life was making a mistake by taking away what was precious to them. They were fully present to their sadness, allowing it to move through them—free of any resistance to life's perfect unfolding.

> … it's natural for feelings to
> arise and fall. Just allow it all.
>
> *Arjuna Ardagh*

Inviting Curiosity Rather Than Judgment

All our feelings deserve to be held without judgment. It's easy to feel gratitude for such emotions as happiness, joy, satisfaction and contentment; however, emotions on the other end of the scale like frustration, impatience, anger, sadness, and resentment are often judged as something unwelcome that we need to push away.

Not wanting to experience those emotions, we might say *no* to feeling them, either denying what we're feeling or the reverse, waging war with them. Another less than healing path is to become a victim and drown in our feelings, singing a tale of woe to all who will listen—in effect building a monument to our distress, wailing in worship of its power over us.

Each of these actions is the result of believing in a story of life's imperfection. However, there is a path we can take that is not informed by such a story. That path is to open our arms to the emotions we are feeling, being fully present to them as we allow them the opportunity to gracefully soften and dissipate. If, as the saying goes, "What we resist, persists," then would not the opposite also hold true, "What we allow, dissolves?"

When we allow a dark emotion the freedom to move within us, what can happen is that the emotion wafts away and a sense of spaciousness takes its place. Understandably, to relax and remain tender—rather than resist and harden—when we're feeling dark emotions is counterintuitive if we've not felt the peace that comes from embracing them. We're so used to pushing away anything unpleasant that the idea of leaning into rather than away from feelings we're *dis*easing ourselves over doesn't make sense. To relax with those feelings may take some measure of resolve coupled with an openness to experiment.

Keep in mind that when we have feelings we want to release, it's essential to question our belief in any story we might be telling ourselves that those feelings don't belong. Instead of labeling those feelings as a mistake, we can see them as important messengers that when welcomed can give us valuable guidance. As the poet Rumi wrote...

> This human being is a guest house.
> Every morning a new arrival.
>
> A joy, a depression, a meanness,
> Some momentary awareness
> comes as an unexpected visitor.
>
> Welcome and entertain them all....
>
> The dark thought, the shame, the malice,
> meet them at the door laughing,
> and invite them in.
>
> Be grateful for whoever comes,
> because each has been sent
> as a guide from beyond.

When we welcome all of our feelings and don't try to elbow them out of the way or helplessly drown in them, we open ourselves to the wisdom they have to offer. Let's say feelings of anger are coursing through us; we can practice being with them from a place of curiosity rather than judgment. In a spirit of curiosity we can ask, *"What's this anger about?"* Then listen for the response.

For instance, a few years ago I was experiencing strong waves of anger. When I asked the question "What is this anger about?" the response I received came in the form of strikingly clear images from my childhood, where I saw myself in circumstances that I viewed through my young eyes as oppressive. From those images I recognized that I was activating within myself, as an adult, a wound that formed when I was very young. The present day situation that I thought was the cause of my anger was a trigger for feelings from decades ago that I'd not yet effectively dealt with as an adult. With that insight—which came from embracing my anger with the "What's this about?" question—I was able to respond to the present day situation in a fresh, mature, responsive way. I saw that my anger was a messenger, extending an invitation to heal a wound from my past. Once I acknowledged the message the anger offered, it was replaced with serenity and confidence.

In every moment we can take the step to welcome with gratitude and curiosity, or to dismiss with disdain and judgment each of the guests Rumi speaks of that will arrive in our lives. How do we want to respond? Are we open to inviting all of our feelings into our house and learning from them, or do we keep ourselves in a state of red alert, standing guard against emotions that we judge shouldn't be knocking at our door?

That said, it's understandable that our reaction to distressing emotions would be to get rid of them. We need to be mindful of not judging ourselves for having that reaction: *"How unspiritual of me to resist any of my feelings; I should be welcoming all of them."* Entertaining such a thought puts us in the land of illusion, given that our resistance to our feelings is *what is* in the moment. Judging ourselves as lacking by believing we shouldn't resist any of our feelings will only exacerbate our distress.

Instead of judging ourselves when we are in resistance to our emotions, a better course to take is to allow our resistance. Saying *yes* to our resistance frees us from believing in a story that it shouldn't be there. In that freedom we give our resistance the space to move on its way, like clouds in the sky.

It's important to remind ourselves that all of our feelings are deserving of our embrace and that the way we are responding to life in any moment is what is—perfect as it is. By allowing ourselves to be as we are and by welcoming all the feelings we're having, we remind ourselves that we can—when the moment feels appropriate—respond to life in a manner that feels graceful and freeing rather than restrictive and stressful.

> One day fear showed up, and I heard thought say, "Fear? What is fear doing here?" Then I heard wisdom say, "Fear is welcome here." I went, "Oh, I see, everything is welcome, everything."
>
> *Pamela Wilson*

Giving Up the Search

A question most people on a spiritual quest ask is, "How can I achieve a lasting peace—a peace unaffected by life's tribulations?" Or as St. Paul put it, "The peace that surpasses all understanding." The answer the world's great spiritual traditions offer is that, first of all, peace isn't something that can be achieved; peace is something we already are, not something missing that we have to seek. Paradoxically, only when we give up searching for peace can we experience peace. Holding a view that peace is something to be attained acts as a roadblock to the peace that is already present.

It's like someone searching his house for his reading glasses when they are already sitting on top of his head. He thinks he has to seek after what is already present. Only when he realizes that he is in possession of his glasses can he relax and release his search. It could be said he is at one with his glasses. There is no *he* separate from *his glasses*. Likewise there is no *you* separate from *the peace that you already are*. You're just in error believing that peace can be somewhere else, separate from you.

Peace is like the rays of the sun bathing us. Thoughts we entertain like, "I should be feeling peace instead of distress," act like clouds blocking the light. Peace hasn't gone anywhere; instead, through our misguided thinking we have clouded peace from our view. Peace isn't an experience we can grasp hold of and keep clasped tightly to our breast; rather, peace is something that is already perfectly present once we stop giving energy to thoughts that cloud our peace.

You'll sometimes hear the notion that to live in peace one needs to renounce thought—that our thinking is what causes us distress. Thinking is not the problem. Planning a vacation requires thinking, nothing wrong with that. However, continually worrying about terrorists attacking us while on vacation is the kind of *dis*easing story-making—"There shouldn't be terrorists"—that walls us off from peace.

> A basic spiritual principal is learning to accept "what is" instead of insisting life be a certain way. Life is rarely the way we want it to be; it's just the way it is.
>
> Robert A. Johnson & Jerry M. Ruhl

This doesn't mean that we're to throw all caution to the wind. Tempting fate by crossing a busy midtown street during rush hour against a flashing *Do Not Walk* signal is simply being reckless. We would do well—in both spirit and body—to still attend to our common sense. With that caveat in mind, we can access the peace of our True Nature by noticing any thought we are having when stressed and ask, "With this thought, what story am I believing in that is blocking my experience of peace?"

The great Indian sage Ramana Maharshi said:

> "It is as it is. That is all you can say."

What Ramana Maharshi points to is the futility of believing in thoughts that take issue with life's expression. Life unfolds as it unfolds. Why suffer by entering into a no-win wrestling match with life, telling ourselves stories that aren't even true?

Responding from a Grateful Heart

It's easy to believe that peace is always available to us when life is unfolding as we'd like. It's not so easy to believe when life doesn't seem to be on our side. Nonetheless, peace is readily at hand even in situations that call up in us anything but peaceful feelings. Let me offer an example.

    I had just finished spending a good deal of money having a roofer replace my home's leaky roof. During the next heavy rainfall, I found a stream of water coming into my kitchen over the stove. My initial reaction was intense contraction, with waves of angry energy moving through me as I put a large pot under the stream of water. At that moment I was not in a place where I could say "Yes, this too!"—especially a *yes* to a leaking roof that I just had replaced.

I sensed that my most appropriate response at that moment was to allow space for my feelings to stomp around a bit. It wouldn't have been helpful for me to try to get rid of my anger and frustration. The timing wasn't right. I embraced my upset. At the same time I recognized that I didn't want to stay in this agitated, reactive state. I wanted to become more responsive to the situation rather than reactive.

To help gain perspective, I reminded myself that I was giving the situation all the meaning it had for me; I was the one responsible for my feelings, not the roofer. Once I gave up my resistance to being upset, I was able to access a calmer state of mind, which led me to ask the question, *"What thought am I believing that is causing my suffering?"*

The answer I got was that my roof shouldn't be leaking, and that the roofer should have been more competent in fixing my roof. Then I acknowledged that with that story I was resisting what is, in effect living in an illusion because my roof was indeed leaking and because the roofer had been as competent—or incompetent—as he was. What could be more insane than to argue with what is? Would my urge to indulge in make-wrong repair my leaking roof? With these questions in mind, I asked myself...

> *Do I want to argue with what is
> and live in a fantasy, inflicting
> suffering on myself?*

or

> *Do I want to see the perfection
> of what is and be at peace?*

Once I resolved that I genuinely wanted peace, I centered myself in my heart by remembering the many things I have to be grateful for in my life: my health, my family, my friends. By gently staying focused on what I could appreciate in my life, I turned my attention in a different direction and the tumultuous feelings began to step back from center stage. Once in this relaxed, appreciative heart space, I asked:

> *How might I respond in this
> situation from my heart?*

Immediately I got an answer: *I could respond by staying relaxed and not get caught up in a drama; I could remember that life unfolds perfectly—there are no mistakes.* By relaxing and by affirming the perfection of life, I couldn't continue to be in my story of *this shouldn't be happening*. I was then able to leave a drama-free phone message for the roofer, calmly explaining the situation.

I stayed in that peaceful place...for about five minutes. Then judgments began to loom again. I once more centered myself in my heart, asking myself what I could appreciate in my life. What came to mind was that I have a house that I love, that the roofer has been responsive in the past when I called with a roofing problem, and that nothing seemed to be significantly damaged by the water. I also focused on other factors in my life not even related to the roof that I felt grateful for, such as my good health, a reliable car, my computer that has rarely given me trouble. In short, I acknowledged all those things in my life that weren't "leaking."

What I found was that through my focus on what I could appreciate in my life, I was able to again get myself into a relaxed, centered place. But after awhile, I found myself tightening up again. I said to myself *Yes, I'm still feeling angry and frustrated*, and then returned to focusing on what I could be grateful for—however not in an attempt to wage a frontal assault to banish my feelings. There was nothing wrong with the anger and frustration. I understood that my amygdala—the part of the brain where anxiety is registered—was trying in its primitive way to exercise me into action. It wouldn't have helped to harden against those feelings and judge them as wrong.

I continued to do the process of acknowledging my anger and frustration and then turning my attention towards what I could appreciate until I found myself firmly rooted in my heart. When my roofer showed up to fix the leak, I was able to be with him without holding any judgmental, blaming energy.

> Everyday, at the moment when things get edgy, we can just ask ourselves, "Am I going to practice peace, or am I going to war?"
>
> *Pema Chödrön*

Now you may be saying to yourself that I had every right to take the roofer to task, letting him know (as if he didn't already) that he'd been lax in his work. And for most of my life I would have agreed with you. I was raised in a home and instructed in a school system addicted to making up a wide range of wrong-making stories: *You should be different. Others should be different. Life should be different. And if you, others, life don't change—and change quickly—then there are consequences to be paid.* In short, *you, others, life need to be fixed.*

At the time I was growing up—and to a great extent today—society gave all the signs of being hooked on wrong-making and blaming. Consider what is shown on TV and in our movies: dramas rooted in the dualities of right-wrong, good-bad. Additionally, most newspapers and magazines understand that their circulation increases with stories that prompt our *ain't it awful* head shaking.

I'm not here to bash the media, the nature of our schools, or how parents choose to raise their children. That gets us nowhere. However, what can be helpful is to recognize the dynamics that influence our perspective of the world and, in turn, our response to it. With greater clarity about the forces shaping our views, we can question our judgmental stories about life.

That said, refraining from judgment doesn't mean one would never learn from experience. For instance, I doubt that I'd hire again the roofer in my example or that I would recommend him to anyone. The point is that I act from a place of discernment rather than wrong-making.

With this in view, be wary of thinking that acting with discernment makes one a "better" person. Avoid going into a story that says "Look at how spiritually awake I am by not making anyone wrong." Or the reverse story, "Oh, how unenlightened I am to be trapped in judgment." Neither story is helpful. Instead, you might hold a perspective like "I'm getting clearer on how to be with distressing feelings so that I can experience peace."

Saying the Yes of Peace

Yes can be one of the most powerfully transforming words to support us in living the perfect peace of our True Nature. The *yes* that I'm pointing to is not a *yes* that signifies approval of world events, personal circumstances or people's behaviors that aren't in line with your values or beliefs. Nor is it the kind of *yes* said haltingly when you're asked to do something you'd prefer not to. Certainly not the *yes* of permitting others to act in such a way that you give yourself feelings that can range from flashes of lip-tightening annoyance to foot-stomping anger.

What is the character of the *yes* I'm speaking about here? It's a *yes* that supports us to live the peace that is always at hand when we allow *what is*, rather than stepping onto a judgmental good-bad, right-wrong, should-shouldn't path of resistance if life fails to meet our expectations. Further, this *yes* can have us saying a *no* to others' requests when we feel called to spend our time differently than they would like. This *yes* supports us in setting appropriate boundaries with others from a centered place of wisdom and appreciation. This *yes* is about taking inspired action from a relaxed and grateful heart that accepts the present moment as it is, rather than taking action from a mind too frequently poised for struggle.

> Whatever comes, you say
> yes to; and whatever goes,
> you say yes to. That is what
> frees up your energy.
>
> *Nirmala*

It's important to understand this view of *yes*, given that one might assume saying *yes* to life means becoming something like a blank slate, eschewing any discernment or action. Not so. This *yes* is advocating the opposite. It's a *yes* responding from a heart that values appreciation over criticism; intimacy over separation. We can have our heart become the wellspring of our actions instead of a constricted, story-making mind, which often is tainted by regrets of the past and concerns about the future.

The nature of the judging mind is to be on *s*urvival alert—ready to fight when it suspects life isn't satisfying our desires. Feelings of *dis*ease, such as anger, frustration and fear are some of the judging mind's more prominent hallmarks.

Saying *yes* to life doesn't mean we rid ourselves of having preferences. That would be denying our very humanity. Rather, we acknowledge and respect our preferences, but do not become a hostage to them. We hold our preferences lightly instead of with an iron fist.

Also, it's important to genuinely feel whatever feelings of contraction come up when challenges enter our lives. We need to give appropriate voice to our suffering, not repress it. When you have a feeling you don't want, say *yes* to it with tenderness. This allows the feeling to move on its way rather than become stuck in your body and emotional field. In this way you regain the perfect peace of your True Nature—which was never really lost, just hidden from your view.

If I am feeling something
and I see that I don't like
it, then I embrace that I
am feeling something
and I embrace the fact
that I don't like it.

A. H. Almaas

Musings

We become a prisoner when chained
to our likes and dislikes.

When feeling distressed, experiment with asking, "What should story am I telling myself that is blocking my peace?" You might surprise yourself with a laugh and return to sanity.

Be encouraged, knowing that to surrender——allowing life to be as it is——is doable in every moment. You can embrace everything in your life with a *yes*.

Being relaxed and open to whatever comes your way provides the grace to see nothing wrong with any life experience——no matter how challenging.

There's no getting around it…stories happen——such as "This is good, this is bad; you should, you shouldn't; I'm worthy, I'm unworthy." If you see these stories as real, rather than fantasies, life becomes very problematic.

What is meant by freedom? Having no concerns that life might not show up the way you want, because you know that you'll always say *yes* to whatever does show up.

Action taken by recognizing that life is perfect as it is will be of a much different quality from action taken with a belief that life makes mistakes. Grace and ease mark the first; stress and struggle mark the second.

When one is awake, there is this gentle, spacious "Yes, thank you!" for life in all its wide variety.

While it's true that no one deserves to be made wrong, a deeper truth is that making anyone wrong is absurd since life is perfect in its expression.

If someone directs wrong-making energy towards me and I react by directing similar energy back, I most probably have wrong-making energy alive within me. There's a saying "You spot it, you got it." If I didn't have wrong-making energy stirring inside, I would be able to remain at peace, regardless of another's attempt to make me wrong. And so the task ahead is clear: clean up my own wrong-making energy.

III

The Three-Step Process for Perfect Peace

Be master of the mind
rather than mastered by mind.

Zen proverb

Removing Barriers to Peace

What the Buddha called "suffering" is our being dissatisfied with life's unfoldment. Indeed, we invite suffering into our experience by believing our stress-producing stories that argue with life. You can use the following three-step process to assist you in identifying those stories, as well as support you in moving from the judging mind to a grateful heart.

As you work with this process, it's important to remember that peace has never left: it is always at hand.

The three-step process helps to remove those barriers that keep you from feeling the perfect peace of your True Nature.

> True investigation is
> designed to reveal what is
> real and what is illusion…
>
> *Gangaji*

The Three-Step Process for Perfect Peace:

Waking Up from the Illusion that Life Should Be Different Than It Is

Step 1: Identify and examine the story at the root of your suffering. Ask yourself:

What story am I telling myself that claims life should be different than it is?

Here are some examples: My husband should be more considerate. Politicians should be honest. I should be making more money at my job. That driver ahead of me should be going faster. Or you may have the story framed with a shouldn't, such as, the driver ahead of me shouldn't be driving so slowly.

Life should be different stories can also contain words like need and ought: My friend needs to be more understanding. I ought to be more assertive.

Further, stories in the form of a wish, such as, I wish my husband were more considerate or "why" questions, such as, why is this happening to me? often have at their core a belief that someone or something should be different.

After identifying your story in this first step, examine the unreality of it by acknowledging that when you resist life with your stories you live in an illusion. For example, you might say to yourself something like this: "The story I'm telling myself argues with life; I suffer when I believe that story because life is always the way it is."

Another way you can acknowledge that you're living in an illusion is to state the reality of the situation. For example:

> *My husband is as considerate as he is—no more, no less. Politicians are as honest as they are right now. At this moment, I'm making the amount of money at my job that I'm making. The driver ahead of me is driving at the speed he is driving—that's what is.*

It can also be helpful to consider what life experience you want to give yourself. You might ask:

> *Do I want to continue my suffering by believing a story that isn't true?*

or

*Do I want to experience the peace
that comes from releasing this story?*

To help answer these questions, imagine how you would feel if you didn't see the story as true. Ask yourself:

*What would I be feeling if I
didn't believe this story?*

Might you be relaxed? Clear-headed? Calm?

Once you've identified and examined the story that is at the root of your suffering, move on to Step 2.

> There is an error in the word 'should', which represents the hypothetical. The hypothetical is never reality and is actually an idealized abstraction. The hypothetical therefore represents a fantasy.
>
> *David R. Hawkins*

Step 2: Access the wisdom and peace of your True Nature through a grateful heart. Place your attention on your heart area for about ten to fifteen seconds, then bring to mind what you are grateful for in your life (e.g., friends, family, health).

Fully experience what you're thankful for in your life. When you feel centered and relaxed, ask yourself:

How might I respond to this situation with my heart's wisdom?

Or you may find it helpful to ask:

What's this situation/feeling about?

When you get your answer, thank your heart for its response.

> Throughout the history of humankind, the oral and written literature has spoken of the wisdom of listening to our own hearts for guidance.
>
> *John Selby*

Step 3: Take action from a grateful heart. Now that you have your heart's response, you can take action, feeling centered and peaceful, back in resonance with your True Nature. Note that the action you take may not always be outward. Your action could be a resolve to change your perspective with no specific outer action necessary.

And if you choose not to follow what your heart tells you, that's perfect too. Be alert to making yourself wrong by believing one way of acting is somehow inherently or morally better than another way of acting. Remember: Your infinitely loving True Nature is without judgment, embracing life in all its colors.

> Suffering follows a
> negative thought as the
> wheels of a cart follow
> the oxen drawing it.
>
> *Buddhist saying*

Once you become proficient in this process, you'll find the steps happening automatically. If you need to use some or all of the steps more than once in a given situation, see the perfection in that.

Feel free to experiment. Buddha's last words were said to be, "Be a light unto yourself." So use the process in a spirit of curiosity and play, modifying the process as you see fit to best support you in releasing untrue, *dis*easing stories that stand as barriers to your peace.

On the next page is a worksheet to guide you in using this three-step process. You can use a blank notebook to write your answers to the questions offered on the worksheet, or you can make copies of the worksheet and write your answers directly on it. In either case, it's highly recommended to write down your answers to the worksheet questions until the three steps become second nature.

The Three-Step Process for Perfect Peace:

Waking Up from the Illusion that Life Should Be Different Than It Is Worksheet

Step 1: Identify and examine the story at the root of your suffering. Ask yourself *"What story am I telling myself that claims life should be different than it is?"* (e.g., *My children should be more considerate. Life should be fair. I shouldn't be so emotional.*)

What story am I telling myself?

How am I living in an illusion by believing this story?

**What might I be feeling if I
didn't believe this story?**

**Do I want to continue to suffer
by believing this story?**

Step 2: Access the wisdom and peace of your True Nature through a grateful heart. With your attention on your heart, fully experience what you're thankful for in your life and then ask the following:

**How might I respond to this situation
with my heart's wisdom?**

and/or

What's this situation/feeling about?

Thank your heart for its response.

Step 3: Take action from a grateful heart. Now that you have your heart's response, you can take action, feeling centered and peaceful, back in resonance with your True Nature. Note that the action you take may not always be outward. Your action could be a resolve to change your perspective, with no specific outer action necessary.

Musings

The Indian sage Sai Baba condensed his entire teaching
into three words, "Watch your thoughts."
Be vigilant, then, of the stories you tell yourself that
cause suffering, realizing none of them are true.

No energy is more healing and wise than
that of a loving and grateful heart.

The sage doesn't tempt arrogance by trying to
control life. She lives in humility, being a clear, open
channel for life's energy to move through her as her.

The desire to change a circumstance in your
life doesn't cause suffering unless you believe
that circumstance shouldn't be as it is.

Observe with an unprejudiced eye everything that goes
on in life: never being for or against, never grasping at or
pushing away. Only then can peace flow freely into your life.

There is a certain Buddhist teaching that proposes we see our challenges in life as gifts. By embracing the very things we want to resist, we free ourselves from the self-inflicted suffering of needing life to show up in a certain way. This opens us to a peace the egoic mind will never understand.

Put an end to your distress by giving heartfelt thanks for life as life is. It's that simple. If it were more complicated, people would probably pay this notion greater attention.

When awake, all one wants to do is give thanks.

The less you're in confrontation with life, the greater your freedom and peace.

Disappointment is the inevitable "reward" for one's attempts to control life.

IV

The Illusion of Separation

There is no separate self… what is present
is only a false idea of a separate self.

Robert Wolfe

Going Beyond the Words

Two root causes of psychological suffering are:

1. The stories we tell ourselves that argue with life's unfoldment, and
2. believing that we are independent agents in that unfoldment—each of us playing our separate roles.

As the great sage Ramana Maharshi points out, "...the only reality is the Self." When we move through the world as if we're separate entities, we open ourselves to suffering.

It's understandable that a mind habituated to a dualistic worldview has difficulty grasping that we are not apart from life, but rather the totality of life itself. Language, which grows out of this dualistic perspective, can never capture in full that which is nondual—the infinite oneness of our True Nature. You're invited, therefore, to go beyond the words offered here on the illusion of separation, allowing whatever insights about the mystery of our *not two* True Nature to emerge in life's perfect timing.

> When one realizes that one
> is the universe, complete
> and at one with All That Is,
> forever without end, no
> further suffering is possible.
>
> *David R. Hawkins*

Knowing Our Oneness

The peace of your True Nature is untouched by any judgmental stories you might tell yourself, such as, *I should be more spiritual, compassionate, enlightened. Others should be kinder, more considerate, loving. Life should be fairer, more peaceful and abundant for all.*

In its oneness, your True Nature is story free. How could your True Nature have a story about anything, since it is everything? There's nothing outside of itself to make up a story about. There is no reference point other than itself, and thus nothing to reference itself to. Further, it's impossible for your True Nature to banish anything from itself or resist anything within itself because there is nothing that is not itself. And that includes "you." (*You* appears in quotation marks for the next few sentences to indicate the illusion of a "you" as separate from life.)

"You" *are* the Oneness, even though it appears to "you" that "you" are a separate being, with free will and choice. What is really happening is that life is flowing through "you" as an instrument of True Nature. "You" think "you" are an agent of action in the world, but it's True Nature that moves through "you," as "you."

The Buddha is noted as saying, "Events happen. Deeds are done. There is no individual doer thereof." Indeed, how most everyone believes the world operates isn't true. We aren't separate individuals orchestrating action in this dream world we call reality. We are not the initiators of action in life; we don't choose anything. Life happens through us and then we put an interpretation onto it, which creates the story that we did this or that by our own choosing.

Even if one is deeply familiar with the concept of enlightenment, the idea that one is "being lived" and has never made an independent decision or choice in one's life may well bring some resistance.

James Braha

Looking Past Appearances

What research studies of brain activity have found is that action precedes thought by a fraction of a second. David R. Hawkins, a leading authority in consciousness, points out that one's thought to take a specific action "happens 1/10,000th of a second *after* the phenomenon [action] has already occurred."

In effect, one takes an action, and what follows that action is the thought about taking the action. For example, I go to get a coat out of my closet: the action of my going to the closet for my coat actually happens *prior to* my having the thought "I think I'll get my coat." Action happens before our conscious decision to take the action.

The notion that action *precedes* thought, and that there is no separate person making choices, is so counter to what most people believe that they dismiss this out of hand or blank out, unable to absorb what's being said. (People five hundred years ago probably had similar reactions to the idea that the earth is round, not flat, and that it circles the sun.)

When I first read an article on nonduality that presented the idea that life happens through us and that we aren't agents of choice in our lives, I couldn't take it in. I knew I was reading English, but the words didn't compute. About a year later I was sorting through a pile of magazines and happened upon this same article. For no particular reason I began to reread the article, and something surprising happened: I felt a powerful resonance with what was being said—as if a thick fog had cleared away.

Why did I understand the article now? Where did this understanding come from? I had no answer. It was as if grace had moved through me, opening my eyes to the possibility that the world isn't as it appears.

Being Lived by Life

Excited about the perspective offered in the article, I made a couple copies for friends. Their response after reading the article was a tepid, "how interesting." That's understandable, given that the dualistic worldview is so pervasive. Either one feels a resonance, or not, with the perspective that we are lived by life and aren't separate individuals acting of our own volition.

The nondual view of life isn't something that can be understood as truth by the mind alone. The mind is focused on creating strategies to ensure the survival of the body, which is perceived as a separate entity that needs protecting. The mind is principally conditioned to determine which actions the body can take to get what the mind thinks the body must have for its survival.

To say that the mind isn't in the lead position with thoughts about what needs to happen for survival, but rather interprets an action *after* the action has taken place, is revolutionary. The mind is dethroned as the prime mover of action, and is reduced to being a witness that doesn't realize it's only a witness. Put another way, the mind has been removed from behind the wheel of the car and is now in the passenger seat.

To further distress the mind, let's consider that, in truth, there isn't anyone behind the wheel either, driving the car. To the mind, that means the car is careening along on its own, with no one in control. No "doer" anywhere.

> What must be emphasized, rather than I am not the doer—which implies a BIG DOER exists—is that there is no doer, or doing, or done.
>
> Stephen Wolinsky

Identifying No "Me" or "Other"

To the mind, which is genetically wired and socially conditioned to ensure the body's survival, this notion that there is no doer—e.g., a *me* as "doer" or some *divine presence* out there as "doer"—can only lead to disaster. For instance, in continuing with our car analogy…What if there's a big tree that's fallen across the road in the car's path?

Well, since everything is really the One—not two, not subject separate from object—then in our car analogy there isn't anything outside of the One to crash into. (There's no car separate from the tree.) In Oneness there can't be space and time as there is in this illusion of duality.

In Oneness there is no movement from *here-now* (car heading towards the tree) to *there-future* (car crashing into the tree). No space-time, and no separate me with any volition to take action.

What is being said here has the disbelieving mind issuing a red alert. But in fact in the True Nature of Oneness, "we" couldn't be any more safe. Which is not to say that if you're driving down the road one fine day and a fallen tree is directly in your way, you wouldn't slam on the brakes—that is, a conditioned "you" will move as True Nature acts through "you" to hit the brakes.

Don't try to wrap your intellect around this. Only a surrendering to the infinite wisdom of our True Nature can help us appreciate that we are simply the instruments through which our True Nature manifests.

Understandably enough the mind—caught in the illusion of duality—thinks this is utter nonsense; only a deeply felt intuitive sense that goes beyond the conditioned mind can grasp the idea that we are not separate individuals with the capacity to initiate actions by our own volition.

Contemporary sage Ramesh Balsekar tells this story about two women sitting next to each other, as he spoke about our not being the choice makers in our lives. One woman became alarmed to hear she had only the illusion of control in her life, while the other woman voiced what a relief it was to hear that she wasn't orchestrating her life.

> The enlightened sage….
> is at one with all of life….
> without any personal sense
> of being the doer of deeds.
>
> *Adyashanti*

Blaming No One

Given that each person has been born with his or her own distinct personality and has experienced his or her own unique life conditioning, life will move through one person differently than another.

Life will move through one person who has been raised in an environment of distrust in a way that is different from someone raised to trust life. And life will move through one person who has been born with an outgoing, happy-go-lucky disposition differently than someone who was born with a more reserved, cautious nature.

No two people are born with exactly the same disposition, nor do any two people experience precisely the same life conditions; therefore, life manifests through each person differently. What are the implications of this perspective? First, blaming myself, others, or life about what is happening in our lives makes no sense, since nothing is actually under our control, our choosing.

Some robbers break into your house while you're away on vacation and steal most everything of value. If life is simply moving through each of us and we're not the actual initiators of our actions, then the robbers of your house aren't to blame for what "they" did.

That doesn't mean you wouldn't file a police report. Or if the robbers are caught they won't be tried in a court of law, perhaps sentenced and sent to prison. However, given this understanding that no one is a doer of any action, to blame the robbers for what they did as if they were the activating agents of their actions doesn't make any sense. We are all without fault—even the most "wicked" of us. People can be rude, offensive, petty, and vicious while at the same time completely innocent and blameless. Quite a paradox.

> ...if you're driving home tonight...
> and you hit somebody's car
> because they passed a red light,
> even if it's their fault physically,
> in reality it's nobody's fault.
>
> *Robert Adams*

What is being said here is not a call to open the prison gates tomorrow, close the courts of law, and suspend any action in the broader scope of life that smacks of punishment. Sending someone to prison for assault, taking away someone's driver's license for repeated traffic offenses, or terminating someone from a job for excessive absences may be what happens; given how life moves through us, with our network of core beliefs, along with the mores of the culture in which we live.

The point to be considered is the spirit in which we take our actions. Do we cast blame—onto others or ourselves—when there is no basis for blame, considering that life moves through each of us without our volition? Remember, our infinitely loving True Nature of absolute oneness simply is, moving through us without any judgments of good or bad, right or wrong. Therefore, when we make ourselves, others, or life wrong we are out of resonance with our True Nature, and suffering shows up.

Note, too, that if we happen to go into wrong-making, that's not wrong. It simply puts us out of resonance with our True Nature. There is no admonition here that we shouldn't engage in wrong-making. If I happen to be making someone wrong, that's simply what is arising. True Nature says *yes* to all of life, excluding nothing in life, making no judgments about what's good or bad, right or wrong.

Just notice, however, that when we do get mired in our judgments—our wrong-making—we're not in a particularly happy, peaceful place.

Understanding the Limits of Language

We've been speaking about True Nature as if it's a separate object that we can be in resonance with or not in resonance with. Well, that's the only way to language it, given that language is rooted in a dualistic worldview. True Nature isn't an object and "we" a subject. Rather, True Nature is undivided, not two.

There is no subject (*a "me" for instance*) relating to an object (*something other than " me"—e.g., True Nature*). Further, it is only a manner of speaking to say that True Nature is embracing all of life. How can True Nature embrace what it itself is? Can one of your thumbs, for instance, embrace itself?

Language, created to help us move in a dualistic world, fails us here. The finite beings that "we" mistakenly take ourselves to be cannot in words describe the ineffable Oneness of the Infinite—what we truly are—that is beyond all concepts.

> A sudden perception
> that subject and object
> are one will lead you
> to a deeply mysterious,
> wordless understanding.
>
> *Huang-Po*

Providing Pointers

The best that can be done is to provide pointers through our words. What is a pointer? Let's say you're looking at a map of California. No one would claim that the map of California and the actual territory of California are the same. The map is a pointer, a representation—not California itself.

So, too, pointers to our True Nature are simply maps and not the actual territory of our True Nature. To add to the difficulty of even providing pointers is that there is no territory to point to for our True Nature; we need to be careful that our pointers don't bring us back to subject-object duality. Our True Nature, again, is Allness.

This isn't something that our minds, conditioned by our dualistic, physical world, can comprehend.

Those individuals who have been awakened to their True Nature (and by the way there are no separate individuals who can be deemed awakened) all say that it's not something that one can capture in words.

As Ramana Maharshi pointed out: "It is as it is, that is all you can say."

That's as close as language can come to accurately describe our True Nature. Plus, in this pointer by Ramana Maharshi, it's important to understand that there really is no "it." "It" would suggest an object and our True Nature isn't an object. "It" is not something separate from "us."

"We" are "It."

"It" is "Us."

And

"It/Us" is

As "It/Us" is.

You have scores of the great
mystics, coming from all
of the great religions, who
find their true identity to
be none other than the
Source of the whole world.

Douglas E. Harding

Turning Upside-Down

When we talk about being in resonance with, or not being in resonance with our True Nature, that's a pointer to help explain why we suffer when we resist life rather than embrace it. And when our True Nature is given attributes, such as "oneness," or "infinite love" those, too, are pointers only. *Our True Nature, which is beyond conceptualization, can have no attributes.* This is a radical understanding that turns on its head most of what humanity holds as the reality of the world.

Your True Nature is not of space and time; it is beyond any concepts the mind can make up. Your True Nature is not physical: when awakened teachers (and remember there are no awakened teachers) say as a pointer to surrender to the will of your True Nature—or synonyms such as God, Consciousness, Source, Divine Presence—it's important to understand that your True Nature has no will as we might understand it with our finite minds.

Also, a statement of surrender such as "Thy will, not mine be done" is nonsensical from the perspective that there actually isn't a "Thy" out there to surrender to and a "mine" here to do any surrendering. A more helpful view of "surrendering" would be that of resting in what is—relaxing with life rather than resisting life.

There's only an "isness" that is free of any concept of will as well as free of being a separate entity with the power of volition. Linguistically, given the duality of language, we can't capture the mystery of what's really going on—or more accurately *not* going on.

Again, your True Nature—absent of any attributes or "separateness" that can exercise volition—simply *is*. Also, there is no divine purpose or design that your True Nature has fashioned for this world of illusion. Life simply happens as it happens as the Oneness. And, paradoxically, there's actually nothing happening at all. So we may as well relax with life, releasing all our resistances.

Resisting Nothing

The way we resist life is by believing in mind-created stories that argue with life. A resistance that doesn't make any sense because what we're resisting isn't even "here," nor are "we" here as separate selves from what isn't "here."

I'm not here; you're not here; the world is not here. There's nothing to resist or anyone to do the resisting. So, too, there's nothing to evolve towards; no grand purpose or design afoot; nothing to worry about or anything to judge—no right or wrong, good or bad—because there is nothing to begin with.

Also, there's no reason to try to improve ourselves or urge others to improve themselves (we don't exist, remember, as separate selves). And, too, if we do happen to want to work at improving ourselves that's also perfect! Our True Nature fully embraces that aspiration as it does everything else that arises. So let's relax and let life unfold as it unfolds—and the unfolding might include improving ourselves, or not improving ourselves.

> …whatever we appear
> to be is nothing but
> concept, conditioning.
> Hence there is no point
> in judging, approving or
> disapproving, approximating
> ourselves to an ideal, or
> clinging to anything.
>
> Robert Powell

What "we" are is all that *is*. We are *That*—the totality of all—which is beyond words.

Often spiritual masters speaking about our True Nature wisely advise their listeners to not believe anything they hear because nothing they hear can even begin to approximate the truth of what is happening—which is *not* happening!

Lao Tzu opens the *Tao Te Ching* with the sentence, "The Tao that can be spoken is not the eternal Tao," And then he forges ahead to give his many pointers to the Tao—certainly powerful pointers—however, these pointers are only a representation, an imperfect reflection.

Who "we" really are—our True Nature—is not of space and time. There's no here or there, no past, present or future. Simply an *isness* that is beyond any concepts "we" may try to place on "it."

What appears as our world is an illusion, called by some as *maya*. This dream world has all the substance of a mirage of water in the desert. Do we take the vibrating energy of a mirage seriously once we know it is a mirage? Try to drink from it after we see through its deception? Once we understand that this world we so often take so seriously is a mirage, and that we are all a mirage in this world, then "we" can relax, resting in the full emptiness of life.

Moving Past Dualistic Logic

In Aristotelian logic, something either is (X) or is not (X). For instance, one is *either a man or not a man*. One can't be both or neither, according to Aristotelian logic. However, Nagarjuna, a second century sage who many Buddhists—including the Dalai Lama—honor as the second Buddha, proposed a logic that moves beyond that of Aristotle's. Nagarjuna postulates that the "objects" in our world can more accurately be described as *neither X, nor not X*.

Rather than one being *either a man or not a man* (Aristotelian logic), according to Nagarjuna's view one is *neither a man nor not a man*. Well, if one is neither a man nor not a man, what is one? Here the mind, which strives for certainty and the known, short-circuits. Silence can be the only answer, a spacious openness.

> Silence is the root
> of everything.
>
> *Rumi*

What Nagarjuna points to is the inability to speak the truth of our world in concepts.

Here's another example...in Aristotelian logic, one would say that a person either has free will or doesn't have free will; according to Nagarjuna this is a false view. Nagarjuna would say that one *neither has free will nor does not have free will*. Again, we're left in silence, resting in the unknown—beyond any concepts—in effect, any stories we may make up about life.

With Nagarjuna's *neither* this (X) *nor not* this (X), one could say there is...

> *Neither this person "I," nor*
> *not this person "I"*
>
> *Neither these other people "them,"*
> *nor not these other people "them"*

*Neither this "planet," nor
not this "planet."*

*Neither this "universe," nor
not this "universe."*

And so again, silence is the only response that can be made. With Nagarjuna's neither this (X) nor not this (X), every concept, every story, disappears; and in the place of our concepts, our stories, what can naturally emerge is the notion of a nothingness that is everything.

True words seem paradoxical.

Tao Te Ching

This notion of a *nothingness that is everything* doesn't make sense to the mind that adheres to the illusion of a dualistic world where—in the logic of Aristotle—either something *is* or *is not*. Plus the mind would judge that which *is* or *is not* as either good or bad, depending on what the mind fancies as in the best interests for the survival of a personal "I."

Remember, the mind is wired for the survival of the personal "I." In a *nothingness that is everything* world, survival becomes a moot point and the personal "I" dissolves.

The good news is that what dissolves, along with this personal "I"—this separate self—is suffering. How can "I" stress myself with judgments about how life should or should not be unfolding when "I" understand that "I" am nothing that is everything?

Yet the conditioned mind does not give up easily with the first insightful blush of seeing through the illusion of a separate self. The mind, habituated to judging how life should or should not be unfolding for the best survival of the personal "I," dismisses the notion of a nothingness that is everything as very strange indeed and not worth seriously considering.

And so the concept-creating factory of the mind will push on unabated in the fashioning of a personal "I"—a separate self—unless there's a resolve to step back and continually question the truth of this separate "I" mind construct.

Being Nothing that Is Everything

What you really are, your True Nature, can't be captured by any tapestry of concepts—no matter how expertly woven by the mind. Yet the mind continues to churn out concept after concept about "you"—none of which are the truth of who "you" really are. Who you are is neither this/that nor not this/that. When asked who he was, the Hindu sage Nisargadatta Maharaj said, "nothing perceivable or conceivable."

Indeed, without any concepts to define myself (Caucasian male with a 401K and Ph.D. living in the Southwest) I am stripped of all story descriptors, unanchored and adrift in the unknown, as the unknown.

This notion of living in the unknown as the unknown—as a nothingness that is everything—is anathema to the conditioned mind, which is addicted to the birthing of concepts for the creation of a "known" separate, personal "I"; especially the birthing of those personal "I" stories that it believes bolsters the best chances for the personal "I"s survival.

However, let's not make the mistake of seeing the mind as an adversary. The mind, which thinks it has our best interests at heart, deserves our appreciation for wanting to keep us safe, even though its efforts are oftentimes coming from what we might call a misguided "worried love."

Thank the mind for its good intentions, and at the same time help it to understand that a "worried love" isn't necessary, and that in truth there is no personal "I" that is even "here" to survive; and that what "I" truly am—as well as "you"—is unbounded, unlimited, a perfect ineffable oneness that is nothing and everything.

That said, if you're walking in a forest and you see a large tree falling in your direction....*move!* Your egoic, dualistic mind is very much at your service by giving a warning that you—being separate from the tree in this relative reality—are in danger of literally becoming one with the tree. Our dualistic perceptions—active in the left hemisphere of the brain—are important to attend to for many instances in life. To see the tree falling your way, and to say to yourself from a nondualistic, right hemisphere brain, *"I am one with the universe, beyond space and time, beyond cause and effect, perfectly safe no matter what,"* wouldn't be health enhancing.

Your True Nature, which is transcendent of duality and nonduality also embraces duality and nonduality equally. What your True Nature gifts you with is the wisdom to dance with both. Indeed, don't fall into the trap of believing that being in a state of nonduality—no matter how blissful—is somehow better than being in a state of duality. (For example, nonduality probably won't be of much help to you in filling out your tax return.) Your True Nature honors both the dual and nondual, while identifying with neither.

Seeing the World as Illusion

To speak metaphorically, one's True Nature is the unchanging screen upon which the movie of life plays out its everchanging stories of heartaches and joys. That unmoving and infinite backdrop of one's True Nature—transcendent, concept-free and absent of any judgmental stories—allows for the flickering, ephemeral images and illusory personal "I" concepts to do the dance of *maya* upon it.

To say life is an illusion doesn't mean that the universe and you and I don't in a sense exist. Rather, the illusion is our interpretation of existence—the stories we make up about it from a place of separation. None of those stories are true. All that you experience is filtered through your conditioned mind. As neuroscientist Candace Pert writes, "...there isn't any absolute or external reality. What you experience is your story of what happened." Put another way, the poet William Blake observed with a sting of pessimism that "man has closed himself up, till he sees all things thro' narrow chinks of his cavern."

So beauty—or any other quality—truly is in the eye of the beholder. The story of beauty that one makes up about some "thing" in life can be a story of indifference or ugliness to someone else. It's our relationship to the things of the world that we create, based on our interpretations—that is the story, the illusion. As the poet Muriel Rukeyser puts it, "The world is made up of stories, not atoms."

Now, making up stories—conceptualizing—isn't the cause of our suffering. To be practical we need to move through our world and relate to the things in it. Concepts based on our interpretations are necessary.

How else, for example, could I communicate to someone that I want to sell my car if I don't conceptualize in language "car." I'd just have to stand there mute. It's only when we believe that our stories, our concepts, are true—an accurate representation of the territory of external reality and not simply a map of that territory—that we lay the foundation for our suffering.

So for practicality's sake I hold that the car I want to sell is definitely there and speak my story (my concept) about the car's value—effectively employing my dualistic self. A person wanting to buy the car may have a completely different story about its value, believing its value is significantly lower than the story I'm proposing. If each of us holds as absolutely true the stories we have about the car's value, then a negotiation will fail and the sale won't happen.

Indeed, if we each have a strong attachment to our differing stories, we will most likely think our story is right and the other person's story is wrong. We might also make up a story about how the other person should see our story as right and their story as wrong.

To go further down this path, if I make up another story—a story that the other person is trying to manipulate me with her story about my car's value—I may fashion an additional story that she isn't playing fair. The possible result: I cause myself suffering—perhaps irritation or anger—because of a belief I have that people should play fair in buying and selling situations—especially with someone as nice and reasonable and as fair as me. I might believe as well in a story that it's my responsibility to tell other people about how unfair she is. (My dualistic self is definitely not serving me well here!)

Let's say she hears from someone my disparaging comments; might she, in turn make up a story that I shouldn't be speaking poorly of her and in her suffering begin telling unflattering stories about me that she holds as 100% true? And so it goes, each of us thinking we have the truth on our side, when all we have is our made-up stories, our tangle of hurtful concepts.

In this way the world is an illusion that we create, and if we're not aware of how the world is an illusion by our relationship to it through our interpretations, we can easily fall into believing our stories. Look at any conflict in your own life or in the world and you'll find people believing in the reality of their differing stories, not understanding that their stories are simply an illusion, an interpretation that is not a reliable purveyor of truth.

> When thoughts arise to interpret an experience as if it should not be happening, or as if it should be different than the way it is, recognize this for what it is—a dream of thought. It's an interpretation. It isn't reality.
>
> *Scott Kiloby*

Losing Our Attachments

If for nothing else but for the sake of practicality, let's take existence as real. You might say that existence is a mass of vibrating energy that forms into configurations of energy that "we" then interpret in a specific way, given our particular sensory apparatus and conditioning. That is the illusion—our interpretation of existence, our filtering of it into stories from the vantage point of a separate self.

Once we get that all is an appearance only, given shape in our minds, our attachment to things being a certain way can't help but loosen up; gain and loss become the same; attachments exit from the stage. Indeed, how can anything be taken personally that is not real—a mirage? And that includes every one of us.

Now these configurations—or forms—of vibrating energy, which we are for the purposes of this discussion taking as real, are not separate from the infinity of vibrating energy that gave them "birth," just as the waves of the ocean are not separate from the ocean. The essence of both is water. One might say—informed by the work of physicist David Bohm—that there is an explicit order (waves of water) and an implicit order (ocean of water).

We, Deepak Chopra suggests, share in the "quantum soup" of existence. We are truly not two, not separate. Separation is an illusion, an interpretation that is false. There is no separate "I" from "you." The story of a separate "I" is not true in the absolute sense. Existence, considered as vibrating energies, is real, while our interpretations—our stories—about this vibrating energy are not. Our conceptualizations are the illusion.

Shining Perfect Peace

If this discussion about what is illusion and what is reality has proven to be tough sledding, put it aside. You don't need to understand what's being presented here to relieve yourself of suffering.

All you need do is to see through the illusion of your stories that argue with life. It may also prove helpful to take to heart this pointer: there is no life happening other than what is happening in our imaginations. In so doing, what can fall away is our attachment to taking positions in life—specifically our should/shouldn't, right/wrong, good/bad judgments. Then the perfect peace of our True Nature has a chance of shining through in our lives, unclouded by our mind-created stories.

Musings

A root cause of our discontent is a belief in the illusion that we are separate from the whole of life. Once we see past this illusion and know that we are at one with the totality of being——which is beyond space, time and description——then discontent dissolves.

You become a blessing to the world when you rest in the infinite love and oneness of your True Nature.

Whether we see an event or person as a blessing or not depends on how we filter reality through our beliefs. Changing our beliefs changes our reality. There is no absolute reality as such——only our stories about reality. And our beliefs are destined to constrict us unless we see them as self-created mental constructs that can be subject to alteration in an eye blink.

I'm neither enlightened nor not enlightened. The same holds for everyone. Enlightenment is simply a pointer to that which cannot be expressed.

Free yourself in the knowing that life is as life is. It isn't good or bad, fair or unfair, buoyant or heavy, friendly or unfriendly, gentle or harsh. Life is none of those things or any other descriptive labeling. Life is as life is——no more to be said.

I find that I'm most awake when I'm fully surrendered to the intelligence of All That Is——this infinite intelligence that I am. There's no "me" apart from the infinite intelligence. There's not the slightest separation, just as the flame is not separate from the fire. All the mystics know how impossible it is to speak about this mystery of the not-two of Oneness.

Living in the unknown, beyond stories, doesn't mean that in this dream world we can ignore such things as gravity, and try flying off cliffs with a flapping of our arms.

Only one life is being lived.

V

Questions and Answers

…when you awaken to your true nature, everything becomes perfectly clear. You're at peace. If something works out, it works out. If it doesn't, it doesn't.

Robert Adams

Question: I'm experiencing more peace as I do the three-step worksheets. I'm just wondering how long I'll need to do them before I'm finally free of my stories. I sometimes think I should be making more progress.

Answer: Trust the process and avoid attempts to speed it up or force it. Be watchful of making up any story that says you should be getting better at it. That won't help. Where you are in your ability to release your stories that cause suffering is perfect. Relax as you do the three-step process and remember that you don't need to be fixed.

Q: Sometimes when I'm looking for what I can be grateful for in a situation I'm stressed about, I can't find it.

A: Attempting to see the gift in a difficult situation can be a trap if you still believe the situation should be different than it is. Don't start out looking for something to be grateful for.

First see as untrue the story that is causing the suffering; then focus on your heart, recalling what you can be grateful for in life, whether related to the situation you're working with or not. From your appreciative heart space you can access the wisdom of your True Nature to support you in dealing with the situation in a relaxed and freeing way.

> **Q: Aren't there some things that are just too big to have a quick response of "Yes, this too!"—such as losing a loved one or facing a severe health crisis?**

A: The more often you say "yes" to life, the easier you'll find it is to experience peace with especially big challenges. Don't force yourself to embrace what's happening and don't tell yourself that you should be at peace. Instead allow all the emotions you're feeling to come up, and honor them. Emotions are energy and need to flow, so be sure to breathe into them rather than tightening up. Know that everything in our lives is perfect as it is. Hold in one hand the full range of your emotions, and in the other a trust in the perfection of what is.

There's a story Ram Dass tells about confronting his guru about the troubles he saw in the world. "Look at the horrors in Bengal," said Ram Dass. His guru replied, "Don't you see it's all perfect!" Ram Dass said "Yeah, it's perfect—but it stinks!" What Ram Dass points to is the dance of both acknowledging the perfection of life's overall scheme and also remaining fully sensitive to what hurts our hearts. Our self-inflicted suffering comes when we believe what's unfolding is wrong, bad, evil, or a mistake that *must* be corrected. This doesn't mean one wouldn't take action to bring about change in the world, if feeling called to do that. How Gandhi moved through the world in his non-violent way is an example. So, too, is the Dalai Lama.

Two questions to consider are *Am I taking action from a peaceful place within me?* Or, *Am I taking action from a place of distress, resisting life, saying no to life's unfoldment?*

Q: When I'm experiencing a difficult situation, I can get out of my suffering with the three-step process, but then in a little while I fall right back into the muck.

A: There's nothing wrong with being in the muck. Be with the feelings that are there in an open and tender way. You have the process to help you wake up and feel the peace of your True Nature. Just keep doing the process without any judgment about what you're feeling. A gentle persistence will serve you best.

Q: I've modified the process, and it seems to work better for me now. Is that okay?

A: Change the process in any way that's helpful; it's not sacrosanct. One person I know focuses on feelings of compassion rather than gratitude in the second step of the process. Feelings of compassion work best for him when accessing the wisdom of his heart.

> **Q: Since I've been working on my stories, I find that I'm uneasy spending time with a friend who's very critical and complains a lot. I know not to judge her since she's perfect as she is and that she doesn't need me to fix her. I'm not sure what to do.**

A: It's to be expected that some people with whom we've been friends appear different in our eyes once we've made a commitment to stop our own complaints and criticisms. As you've pointed out, your friend is perfect as she is and doesn't need to be fixed. What you can do is let her know about the commitment you've made to end your suffering.

When speaking with her have no agenda to change her or make her wrong. Trying to school her in life's perfection and her True Nature wouldn't be helpful. However, if you feel she's open to hearing how you move through life, then share this with her, but not from a place of superiority or feeling that she should embrace your way of being. Accept that she lives her life in a way that's perfect for her. As much as possible speak from a loving heart and let your relationship take its natural course.

> **Q: I get the point of saying "yes" to life, but when I listen to the news I wonder if I'm deluding myself into believing that everything that's happening in the world is just fine as it is.**

A: I wouldn't hold that what's happening in the world is "fine," if you're using the word in the sense of a judgment that means good as compared to "not fine," which would be seen as bad.

You may want to take the view that what's happening in the world is simply what's happening in the world—it's neither fine nor not fine—and refrain from any labeling. It's a challenge not to put an interpretation on events. That's what we've done for most of our lives. The world is as it is. And from a place of embracing what is—not meaning that you approve of what is—you can take action from your heart.

Late in his life, the great sage Krishnamurti shared what he called his secret, which was, "I don't mind what happens." He didn't get caught up in stressing himself with what one might interpret as "bad" life events. Notice how free of suffering your life is when you don't believe in stories that are against life; when you don't live in resistance to what is. This is not to suggest that you'll never experience a burst water pipe in your home, have a car accident or health challenges—it's said that the Buddha died of food poisoning. All of life will unfold as it unfolds. The difference is that when you live in non-resistance there's no judgmental story layered on top of any life experience.

You may find it helpful to consider what the Indian sage Nisargadatta Maharaj said: "In my world, nothing ever goes wrong." Nisargadatta lived beyond the duality of right or wrong, good or bad, should or shouldn't. Consider what your life would be like if you lived in a world where you saw nothing going wrong; where you experienced the perfection of life's unfoldment. Would you be friends with life—awake and at peace?

Q: What do you mean when you say there are no awakened teachers? What about the Buddha?

A: No one is awakened because there's no one here to reside in a state called awakened. When the Buddha was asked who he was, he said "awake." He didn't say, "awakened," in the sense of being in some sort of self-identified, blissed-out state. The Indian sage Yogananda said that if someone claims to be awakened that person probably isn't. How can someone claim to be awakened if there's no "I" to be awakened? That's not to say that there aren't what we might interpret as awakening experiences.

Q: What has your experience been with awakening and what did you do to have those experiences?

A: My most significant awakening experience wasn't planned: it happened by grace. I was collaborating with a friend on various projects to assist a non-profit organization be more congruent with its vision. My friend and I worked well together, except for those times when she became edgy and argumentative. When I spoke with her about this, she'd either become defensive or she'd make herself wrong, going into self-pity. After many weeks of mutual frustration, we realized we were at an impasse, and she suggested that we meet with a counselor she had worked with a couple of years earlier who might be able to help us out.

At the start of our initial session with the counselor, I spoke about the behavior of my friend that I found frustrating. The counselor listened to what I said and commented, "Well, that's the way she is." When I heard him say, "That's the way she is," a strong quaking sensation arose inside my chest. I couldn't speak and sat there confused, not able to understand what was happening. The counselor noticed my silence and asked why I had become so quiet. I described the quaking inside me and when it began.

As the counselor and I spoke, I realized that I was the one frustrating myself by believing my friend shouldn't be edgy and argumentative. I was suffering by arguing with what is. What I came to see is that the quaking signaled the breaking apart of the lie that my friend should be different than she is, or that anyone or anything in life should be any different.

I learned from the counselor that if I had feelings, such as anger or frustration, around my friend I could say to her something like, "It's important for me to let you know that I'm feeling a lot of irritation right now with what I experience as our arguing." Rather than make my friend wrong for her behavior, I could describe what was going on for me in a self-responsible way, without being attached to her changing. Once I began speaking in this way, our relationship smoothed out dramatically.

This awakening experience helped me to see what was at the root of my suffering, and be open to learning how to end it. The Buddha said, "I teach one thing, and one thing only. The truth of suffering, and the way out of suffering." Don't get fooled into searching for a nirvana of unending bliss. Devote yourself to the day-to-day work of seeing through the lies we tell ourselves that argue with life. That's the way to peace.

Q: But what if your relationship hadn't improved? What would you have done then?

A: I would first make sure that I'd seen through the story—the illusion—I created that she should be different than she is. After doing that, I would center myself in my heart and ask for guidance. My heart might tell me to step back from working on projects with her, or it might advise to stay in the relationship and focus on blessing her when she became argumentative. There could be any number of answers my heart might give me. All I know for certain is that the heart gives much wiser counsel than the mind, especially a judging mind.

It's important to understand that just because you resolve to come from your heart and not make others wrong, people aren't necessarily going to change to suit you. Life moves through all of us differently, and some relationships would benefit from an adjustment when there's not a way to reach a mutually satisfying way of being with each other.

Q: Do you have any kind of spiritual practice?

A: My spiritual practice is daily living, with a devotion to free myself of stories that argue with life. That way I can stay connected with my heart and bless life as it is. There's a saying that the wise wander freely in this world, carrying only blessings. I find that I'm most wise and awake when I'm blessing life rather than resisting it. I aspire to say "yes" and "thank you" to whatever shows up. Which, paradoxically, might be something I'm resisting. I aspire to say "yes" to that as well. Nothing is excluded.

This "yes" naturally grows out of not believing that there are two powers in the world—that is, good and bad. If I'm experiencing an illness, a disappointment, or a lack in my life, I know that it is simply an illusion: my True Nature is without deficiency or blemish. With this knowing there's no fertile ground for should or shouldn't mental chatter. When I'm in a blessing spirit, affirming the oneness of life, I am at peace, relaxed in the stillness.

> Self-realization means that we have been consciously connected with our source of being. Once we have made this connection, then nothing can go wrong.
>
> *Swami Paramananda*

Musings

There is a creative, ordering intelligence alive in the universe beyond anything we can possibly imagine: To feel distress about how life is unfolding——given our finite mind——makes no sense to those who realize that we can't see the larger picture. Having that understanding doesn't mean one might not shed tears at losing a loved one, or comfort those who experience loss. It's important to respect this mystery of having a human experience in an infinite universe that is always functioning perfectly.

Life is the ultimate surprise party that has one surprise popping up after another——some appealing, some not. We can either join in the party, gracefully dancing with each surprise, or stumble around grasping at those surprises that we like while trying to push those that we don't like out the door.

Contemplate what your world would be like if you sincerely said, "How perfect!" to each and every life experience——rather than judging experiences as good, not so good, or just plain awful.

You can't be laughing and at the same time
believing life should be different than it is. That's
why laughter is so healing——it embodies
the truth that life is all right just as it is.

How peaceful it must be to dislike nothing
in one's life——to see nothing as wrong.

What would your life be like if you took action free
of any fixed agendas and no thoughts of gained
advantage that spring from feelings of not enough?

How often do we stay stuck in our suffering by not
wanting to let go of our stories about life's errant ways?

When your thoughts, words and actions are centered
in your heart, separation has no soil in which to grow.

See the humor in your thinking: as Lao Tzu
advised, "When you have a thought, laugh!"

Resources

Adams, Robert. *Silence of the Heart: Spiritual Dialogues with Robert Adams*. Atlanta, GA: Acropolis Books, 1999.

____ *Silence of the Heart: Spiritual Dialogues with Robert Adams, Vol II*. Sedona, AZ: Robert Adams Infinity Institute, 1992.

Adyashanti. *Emptiness Dancing: Selected Dharma Talks of Adyashanti*. Los Gatos, CA: Open Gate Publishing, 2004.

____ *The Impact of Awakening: Excerpts from the Teachings of Adyashanti*. Los Gatos, CA: Open Gate Publishing, 2000.

Almaas, A. H. *The Unfolding Now: Realizing Your True Nature through the Practice of Presence*. Boston, MA: Shambhala Publications, 2008.

Ardagh, Arjuna Nick. *How About Now: Satsang with Arjuna*. Nevada City, CA: Self X Press, 1999.

____ *Relaxing into Clear Seeing: Interactive Tools in the Service of Self-awakening*. Nevada City: CA: Self X Press, 1999.

Balsekar, Ramesh. *Pointers from Nisargadatta Maharaj*. Durham, NC: The Acorn Press, 1982.

____ *Sin and Guilt: Monstrosity of Mind*. Mumbai, India: Zen Publications, 2000.

Barnett, Raymond. *Relax, You're Already Home*. New York: Penguin, 2004.

Bayda, Ezra. *Being Zen: Bringing Meditation to Life*. Boston: Shambhala, 2002.

Beck, Charlotte Joko. *Nothing Special: Living Zen*. New York: HarperCollins, 1993.

Bennett-Goleman, Tara. *Emotional Alchemy: How the Mind Can Heal the Heart*. New York: Harmony Books, 2001.

Borich, Judy. *Touch and Go: The Nature of Intimacy*. Tijeras, NM: Interact Publishing, 2002.

Brown, Michael. *The Presence Process: A Healing Journey into Present Moment Awareness*. New York: Beauford Books, 2005.

Bruteau, Beatrice. *Radical Optimism: Rooting Ourselves in Reality*. New York: Crossroad Publishing, 1993.

Braha, James. *Living Reality: My Extraordinary Summer with "Sailor" Bob Adamson*. Longboat Key, FL: Hermetician Press, 2006.

Carse, David. *Perfect Brilliant Stillness: Beyond the Individual Self*. Shelburne, VT: Paragate Publishing, 2006.

Chödrön, Pema. *When Things Fall Apart: Heart Advice for Difficult Times*. Boston: Shambhala Publications, 1997.

Cohen, Alan. *Joy Is My Compass: Taking the Risk to Follow Your Bliss*. Somerset, NJ: Alan Cohen Publications, 1990.

Cushnir, Raphael. *Setting Your Heart on Fire: Seven Invitations to Liberate Your Life*. New York: Broadway Books, 2003.

Dalai Lama. *Kindness, Clarity and Insight*. Ithaca, NY: Snow Lion Publications, 1984.

DeMello, Anthony. *Awareness: The Perils and Opportunities of Reality*. New York: Image Books, 1992.

Duncan, Shannon. *Present Moment Awareness: A Simple Step-by-Step Guide to Living in the Now*. Novato, CA: The New World Library, 2001.

Dyer, Wayne. *The Power of Intention: Learning to Co-create Your World Your Way*. Carlsbad, CA: Hay House, 2004.

Dzuiban, Francis Peter. *Consciousness is All: Now Life Is Completely New.* Nevada City, CA: Blue Dolphin Publishing, 2006.

Fenner, Peter. *Radiant Mind: Awakening Unconditioned Awareness.* Boulder, CO: Sounds True, 2007.

Ferrini, Paul. *The Ecstatic Moment: A Practical Manual for Opening Your Heart and Staying in It.* Greenfield, MA: Heartways Press, 1996.

Finley, Guy. *The Essential Laws of Fearless Living: Find the Power to Never Feel Powerless Again.* San Francisco, CA: Weiser Books, 2008.

Ford, Debbie. *The Dark Side of the Light Chasers: Reclaiming Your Power, Creativity, Brilliance and Dreams.* New York: Riverhead Books, 1999.

Foster, Jeff. *Beyond Awakening: The End of the Spiritual Search.* United Kingdom: Non-Duality Press, 2007.

____ *Life without a Centre: Awakening from the Dream of Separation.* United Kingdom: Non-Duality Press, 2006.

Gangaji. *The Diamond in Your Pocket: Discovering Your True Radiance.* Boulder, CO: Sounds True, 2005.

Gill Nathan, *Being: The Bottom Line.* United Kingdom: Non-Duality Press, 2006.

Golas, Thaddeus. *The Lazy Man's Guide to Enlightenment.* New York: Bantam Books, 1971.

Goldsmith, Joel S. *The Art of Spiritual Healing.* San Francisco: HarperCollins, 1959.

____ *Practicing the Presence: The Inspirational Guide to Regaining Meaning and a Sense of Purpose in Your Life.* San Francisco: HarperCollins, 1958.

____ *The Thunder of Silence.* New York: HarperOne, 1961.

Greven, John. *Oneness.* United Kingdom: Non-Duality Press, 2005.

Gyatso, Geshe Kelsang. *Eight Steps to Happiness: The Buddhist Way of Loving Kindness.* London: Tharpa Publications, 2000.

Hallinan, Joseph T. *Why We Make Mistakes: How We Look without Seeing, Forget Things in Seconds, and Are Pretty Sure We Are Way Above Average.* New York: Broadway Books, 2009.

Hamilton, Elizabeth. *Untrain Your Parrot: And Other No-nonsense Instructions on the Path.* Boston: Shambhala, 2007.

Hammerskjold, Dag. *Markings.* New York: Alfred Knopf, 1965.

Harding, Douglas, E. *Face to No-Face: Rediscovering Our Original Nature.* Carlsbad, CA: Inner Directions Publishing, 2000.

Harris, Bill. *Thresholds of the Mind: Your Personal Roadmap to Success, Happiness and Contentment.* Beaverton, OR: Centerpointe Research Institute, 2007.

Hartong, Leo. *Awakening to the Dream: The Gift of Lucid Living.* United Kingdom: Non-Duality Press, 2001.

Harvey, Andrew. *The Direct Path: Creating a Journey to the Divine through the World's Mystical Traditions.* New York: Broadway Books, 2000.

Hawkins, David R. *Transcending the Levels of Consciousness: The Stairway to Enlightenment.* W. Sedona, AZ: Veritas Publishing, 2006.

Hillier, Gina Mazza. *Everything Matters, Nothing Matters: For Women Who Dare to Live with Exquisite Calm, Euphoric Creativity and Divine Clarity.* Pittsburgh: St. Lynne's Press, 2008.

Jenkins, Sara (ed.) *Turning Towards Happiness: Conversations with a Zen Teacher and Her Students.* Lake Junaluska, NC: Present Perfect Books, 1991.

Johnson, Robert A. *Balancing Heaven and Earth: A Memoir.* New York: HarperCollins, 1998.

Johnson, Robert A. & Ruhl, Jerry M. *Contentment: A Way to True Happiness.* San Francisco: HarperSanFrancisco, 1999.

Kersschot, Jan. *Nobody Home: From Belief to Clarity.* United Kingdom: Non-Duality Press, 2003.

Katie, Byron. *Loving What Is: Four Questions that Can Change Your Life.* New York: Harmony Books, 2002.

____ *Who Would You Be without Your Story?* Carlsbad, CA: Hay House, 2008.

Kiloby, Scott. *Love's Quiet Revolution: the End of the Spiritual Search.* BookSurge Publishing, 2008.

____ *Reflections of the One Life: Daily Pointers to Enlightenment.* BookSurge Publishing, 2009.

Klein, Jean. *Be Who You Are.* United Kingdom: Non-Duality Press, 2006.

Kornfield, Jack. *The Wise Heart: A Guide to the Universal Teachings of Buddhist Psychology.* Boulder, CO: Sounds True, 2008.

Levenson, Lester. *No Attachments, No Aversions: The Autobiography of a Master.* Sherman Oaks, CA: Lawrence Crane Enterprises, 2003.

Liquorman, Wayne. *Never Mind: A Journey into Non-duality.* Redondo Beach, CA: Advaita Press, 2004.

Markides, Kyriacos. *The Magic of Strovolos: The Extraordinary World of a Spiritual Healer.* New York: Penguin Books, 1985.

Marvelly, Paula. *The Teachers of One: Living Advaita Conversations on the Nature of Non-duality.* London: Watkins Publishing, 2002.

McKenna, Jed. *Spiritual Enlightenment: The Damnedest Thing.* USA: Wisefool Press, 2002.

____*Spiritual Warfare*. USA: Wisefool Press, 2007.

Mercie, Christine. *Sons of God*. Camarillo, CA: DeVorss Publications, 1954.

Merzel, Dennis Genpo. *Big Mind, Big Heart: Finding Your Way*. Salt Lake City, UT: Big Mind Publishing, 2007.

Misita, Michael. *How to Believe in Nothing and Set Yourself Free*. Malibu, CA: Valley of the Sun Publishing, 1994.

Mitchell, Stephen, trans., *Tao Te Ching*. New York: HarperCollins, 1988.

Nirmala. *Nothing Personal: Seeing beyond the Illusion of a Separate Self*. Prescott, AZ: Endless Satsang Press, 2001.

Nisargadatta M. *I Am That*. Durham, NC: Acorn Press, 1973.

Pert, Candace B. *Everything You Need to Feel Go(o)d*. Carlsbad, CA: Hay House, 2006.

Packer, Toni. *The Silent Question: Meditating in the Stillness of Not-Knowing*. Boston: Shambhala Publications, 2007.

Parsons, Tony. *As It Is: The Open Secret of Spiritual Awakening*. Carlsbad, CA: Inner Directions Publishing, 2000.

____ *Invitation to Awaken: Embracing Our Natural State of Presence*. Carlsbad, CA: Inner Directions, 2004.

Pearsall, Paul. *Making Miracles*. New York: Prentice Hall Press, 1991.

Powell, Robert. *The Real is Unknowable, the Knowable is Unreal*. Berkeley, CA: North Atlantic Books, 2005.

____ *The Ultimate Medicine*. San Diego, CA: Blue Dove Press, 1994.

Prendergast, John J., Fenner, Peter, and Krystal, Shelia, eds. *The Sacred Mirror: Nondual Wisdom and Psychotherapy*. St. Paul MN: Paragon House, 2003.

Remen, Rachel Naomi. *Kitchen Table Wisdom: Stories that Heal*. New York: Riverhead Books, 1996.

Richo, David. *The Five Things We Cannot Change...and the Happiness We Find by Embracing Them*. Boston: Shambhala, 2005.

Robinson, Rita Marie. *Ordinary Women, Extraordinary Wisdom: The Feminine Face of Awakening*. Winchester, UK: O Books, 2007.

Russell, Peter. *From Science to God: A Physicist's Journey into the Mystery of Consciousness*. Novato, CA: New World Library, 2002.

Schmidt, Amy. *Dipa Ma: The Life and Legacy of a Buddhist Master*. New York: Blue Bridge, 2005.

Selby, John. *Quiet Your Mind: An Easy-to-Use Guide to Ending Chronic Worry and Negative Thoughts and Living a Calmer Life*. Novato, CA: New World Library, 2004.

Simone, Cheryl and Vasudev, Sadhguru Jaggi. *Midnights with the Mystic: A Little Guide to Freedom and Bliss*. Charlotte, VA: Hampton Roads Publishing, 2008.

Singer, Michael, A. *The Untethered Soul: The Journey beyond Yourself*. Oakland, CA: New Harbinger Publications, 2007.

Somers, Juli. "Know Thyself." Santa Fe, NM: *The Center for Inner Truth Newsletter*, May/June 2009.

Suzuki, Shunryu. *Zen Mind, Beginner's Mind*. New York: Weatherhill, 1970.

Sylvester, Richard. *The Book of No One: Talks and Dialogues on Non-Duality and Liberation*. United Kingdom: Non-Duality Press, 2008.

Targ, Russell and Hurtak, J.J. *The End of Suffering: Fearless Living in Troubled Times...or, How to Get Out of Hell Free.* Charlottesville, VA: Hampton Roads Publishing, 2006.

Tarrant, John. *Bring Me the Rhinoceros: And Other Zen Koans that Will Save Your Life.* Boston: Shambhala, 2008.

Thondup, Tulku. *Boundless Healing: Meditation Exercises to Enlighten the Mind and Heal the Body.* Boston & London: Shambhala Publications, 2000.

Tolle, Eckhart. *Gateway to Now.* New York: Simon and Schuster, 2003.

____ *Stillness Speaks.* Novato, CA: New World Library, 2003.

Waite, Dennis. *Enlightenment: The Path through the Jungle.* United Kingdom: O books, 2008.

Wilber, Ken. *The Simple Feeling of Being: Embracing Your True Nature.* Boston and London: Shambhala, 2004.

Wolfe, Robert. *Living Nondualitiy: Enlightenment Teachings of Self-Realization.* Ojai, CA: Karina Library, 2009.

Wolinsky, Stephen. *I Am That I Am: A Tribute to Sri Nisargadatta Maharaj.* Capitola, CA: Quantum Institute Press, 2000.

____ *You Are Not: Beyond the Three Veils of Consciousness.* Capitola, CA: Quantum Institute Press, 2002.

Zohar, Dahna. *The Quantum Self: Human Nature and Consciousness Defined by the New Physics.* New York: William Morrow, 1990.

Zukav, Gary. *The Seat of the Soul.* New York: Simon and Schuster, 1989.

About the Author

Ralph Huber's professional background includes educator, corporate trainer, and vice-president of a New York-based management consulting firm that offered services to major communication and retail industries.

He is currently a member of Hummingbird Community in northern New Mexico and serves as board president for the Unity Church in Santa Fe.

Ralph has a Ph.D. from New York University's Department of Communication Arts and Sciences.

He has an affinity for Advaita, Zen and Christian Mysticism.

For information on personal coaching or seminars, contact *awakeningintoperfectpeace.com*

Acknowledgements

Michael Elliott for his encouragement, support, advice and manuscript publishing skills that played a decisive role in refining *Awakening Into Perfect Peace*.

Hummingbird Community, which inspires me to embrace all of life in unity and love.

The Unity Santa Fe spiritual community and its minister, Rev. Brendalyn Batchelor, for the difference made in my life as we live our shared vision of celebrating the oneness and divinity of all creation.

Jake and Hannah Eagle, whose Reology work keeps me awake to the value of speaking with clarity and intimacy.

Marie Ruster, Norma Philipps, and Amanda Creighton for their insightful comments in the preparation of the manuscript.

My deep gratitude to Muse Harbor publishers Ian Wood, Eileen and Dave Workman for their belief in this book and to Matt Pallamary for his valuable editorial suggestions.

www.ingramcontent.com/pod-product-compliance
Lightning Source LLC
Chambersburg PA
CBHW060527100426
42743CB00009B/1450